MISEDUCATION OF THE ALPHA WOMAN

Miseducation of the Alpha Woman

By
Dr. Shekina Farr Moore

Featuring Expert Authors

Aisha N. Martin
Dr. Barbara Swinney
Dr. Koyah Alston
LaToya Rose
Shontavia Hornsby
Stephanie A.
Suprena Hickman

Literacy Moguls books may be purchased for educational, business, or promotional use. For information, please email publishme@literacymoguls.com.

ISBN-13: 978-1-938563-25-6

Published by Literacy Moguls Publishing Co. www.literacymoguls.com

950 Eagles Landing Pkwy, Ste 610 Stockbridge, GA 30281

FIRST EDITION

Dedication

This book is dedicated to every ALPHA woman who has been told she is too much and, therefore, not enough.

Table of Contents

"Alpha women are self-assured, self-reliant high achievers and are typically physically attractive. They don't mess around. Often they are business owners and/or hold multiple degrees. This doesn't mean they are uncompassionate ice queens a la Grace Jones in *Boomerang*. Ironically, they are completely opposite. Alpha Women know how to balance it all with a Coke and a smile. Then again, she tends to be physically fit, so we may have to nix that Coke for a Dasani water."

-BlackandMarriedwithKids.com

Introduction

Miseducation of the Alpha Woman, An Anthology

Look. You've been lied to—well, at least partially lied to. Yes, Alpha women are bosses, pure and simple, but that's only *one* side of our personalities and makeup! Being seen as hard-nosed, intimidating, mercenary women can be upsetting when we really crave compassion, friendship and companionship as much as anybody else.

We have thoughts, feelings, concerns, fears, vulnerabilities just like the next chic. We just don't always feel we can show it. Hello, somebody! But…We'll talk about that in the chapters to come.

We decided to come together to write a book that addresses the miseducation of the Alpha woman. We feel completely misunderstood and we want to set the record straight.

There are realities that we face in our careers as well as in relationships, and we often feel isolated. Here are some reasons why.

Daunting Realities Alpha Women Face:

> ➢ People find us intimidating
> ➢ We sometimes forget to come up for air
> ➢ We are constantly having to prove ourselves
> ➢ We often have to pick up others' slack
> ➢ We care too much about what others' think
> ➢ We have a hard time finding balance
> ➢ We are often seen as the archetype of strength so we have a hard time showing vulnerability/weakness
> ➢ We have a hard time finding a partner who can keep up with/surpass us

And this list just scratches the surface of the landscape for Alpha women. It's not that we're high maintenance, it's that *our standards* are super high. We apply said standards not only to ourselves, but with potential partners, too.

Can we help that we know what we want and how to get it? You know—these qualities seem so attractive to employers, business partners and romantic interests in the beginning but we soon come to find out that the honeymoon period is short-lived.

But why?

Could it be that the masses have been *miseducated*?

The Miseducation of the Alpha Woman Anthology features stories from leading alpha women across the country, and its topics include fascinating stories ranging from alpha women's experiences within Corporate America, to barriers in romantic relationships, to journeys of professional and personal growth.

Elle: How is your marriage to Jay Z?

Beyonce: It's a power struggle. But if I didn't respect someone and they didn't have that strength, then I would be bored. I wouldn't be attracted to them.

"She's on top of her game. She is obstinate, sometimes conceited and doesn't always make it easy for you. She gives you a run for your money and makes you work overtime on her, so to speak. But all this only makes her more appealing to you. She is, in other words, the quintessential "alpha female. The alpha female has an uncanny ability to make men desire her. The alpha female's talents are special, and consequently, satisfying her might be a man's biggest marital challenge yet."

-AskMen.com

The Irresistible Alpha Woman

Alpha Men Desire Alpha Women

By Dr. Shekina Farr Moore

Not all men can handle us, but not *all* men are scared to date and marry us, either. In fact, there is a sector of men who actually prefer and gravitate toward alpha women. Alpha men know and understand the power of our wiles and deep down think they can tame us.

Alpha men sometimes love a challenge and we do that for them. You see this often in the "power couple" dynamic. (Yes! There is hope for you yet.) A power couple consists of two people who are each influential or successful in their own right. Two compatible alphas in a relationship make a power couple.

The challenge with most of these relationships is that when the alpha male courts the alpha female, they love hard but they also butt heads hard. There are times when there is an undeniable power struggle rumbling and neither wants to back down.

Like most women, the Alpha woman desires a strong, masculine, alpha male. However, Alpha males are usually attracted to the opposite of themselves. They want a woman who embodies feminine energy.

As Alpha women who are used to being the bosses and "Queen Bs" in their own worlds, we sometimes find it challenging to be vulnerable in our relationships and/or to allow men to play the roles of protector and provider. But that is who they are.

Real talk, many men don't want to fight at home. They want peace. Likewise, Alpha women don't want to be dictated to, they want open communication and resolve. Hence, the two have to learn to play the game or "dance the dance" in order to make the relationship work.

Therefore, the challenge for Alpha women like myself who are head strong, used to going after what we want, and will *give you the business,* is to "push and pull" within the paradigm of our romantic relationships.

Consider chess, if you will. In the game of chess, the king is the most important piece but he is also one of the weakest. He can only move one square in any direction—up, down, to the sides, and diagonally. The queen, however, is the most powerful piece. She can move in any one direction—forward, backward, sideways, or diagonally. And how *she* moves affects how *he* moves.

Did you catch the difference between the most important and the most powerful? (Hmmm-hmmmm.) You see, you won't be diminished in this. You win in this.

Accept that the energy you exude and the way you approach your Alpha man directly affects his response and behavior, and you can literally have your way. He will find you completely irresistible in and outside of your home. No power is lost and you can put your cape back on when you fly out the window in the morning. (Wink)

You see, we Alpha women are most successful in our love lives when we know when to drive and when to be chauffeured.

When we are on the same page at the same time with our Alpha men, the world around us is in trouble. If we agree to accomplish a particular task and form a united front, we work in perfect harmony as an unbeatable team.

Here are some reasons Alpha men desire Alpha women like you:

> ➤ **We intrigue and challenge them.** What man doesn't love a challenge; a woman who will call him on his ish. Just like not all women desire a *honey-do*, neither do all men.

> ➤ **We are great at making plans.** Because we are on top of things, we make ish happen. Not only will Alpha men enjoy grandeur, they will enjoy the discounts we negotiate for us.

> ➤ **We raise respectful, accomplished children.** We set high standards and expectations because we ourselves abide by them.

➤ **We make great business partners.** Our drive ambition, goal-setting skills and self-efficacy are desirable assets in for a power couple. Because we are risk-takers we chase dreams right alongside our man. Men who seek to build wealth and have vision embrace this and find it rather attractive.

➤ **We have amazing sex.** Hands down. We are confident in our sexuality and make no qualms about making the first or last moves. If we want you, we'll take you. And you will love it. (Wink) Men love it when women initiate.

Here's a challenge from *Science of People*. The next time you are at a party or networking event, try this fascinating experiment:

Find a group of three or more women —you do not need to be close enough to hear them, they just should be in your line of sight. Put a five-minute timer on your phone or watch and take note of the direction of the women's feet.

Almost always, women point their feet toward the person they are most interested in or who they feel is leading the group's tempo. In only five minutes you will be able to see where the majority of the women are pointing their feet.

Amazingly, you will notice that most of the women in the group will be pointing toward the same woman–even if they are in a circle and even if that woman is not talking.

If women do this, what kind of magnetism do you think an Alpha man has to an Alpha woman—*naturally*?

The two of us naturally vibe on many levels. Here are some of the many ways we get down:

> **We both have high standards.**
> He won't accept poor treatment, and neither will you, which is why you'll never feel neglected. You'll both want your relationship to be the best relationship in town, which is why you'll try your hardest to make each other happy.
> **We understand each other's need for space.**
> He won't question you when you go out with your friends, or get upset when you ask him to leave you alone for a few

hours. He'll understand that you need some time to yourself, because he feels the same way.

➤ **We're both passionate.**
An alpha woman plus an alpha male equals the hottest sex you'll ever have. Inside and outside of the bedroom, you'll both put in your all, which means you're bound to have some steamy sex.

➤ **His career comes first, too.**
Some men can't understand your obsession with your career. However, alpha males love their jobs too, so they won't ever tear you down for wanting to put in extra hours at the office.

➤ **He doesn't get caught up in gender roles.**
Real alpha males don't give a damn about gender roles. If you're too busy to cook for him, then he'll whip something up without feeling any less masculine than he did before.

➤ **He doesn't need a relationship to feel fulfilled.**
This might not sound like a good thing, but it certainly is. It means he's dating you, because he wants to date you, and not because he feels like he needs any old woman in his life.

➤ **He can take a joke.**

Alpha males have high confidence, so they won't get emotional when you poke fun at them. They'll be able to handle the borderline inappropriate jokes that some alpha women love to make.

➢ **He appreciates your feisty personality.**
Some men are scared off by an alpha woman's bold traits. However, your personality isn't unappealing to him—it's actually incredibly sexy.

➢ **He's used to hard work.**
Serious relationships require plenty of effort, but that won't scare an alpha male away. He's used to working hard, just like you are, so he'll see the challenge as a positive thing.

➢ **We'll grow together.**
We're both intelligent, which means we'll have a lot to teach each other. A healthy relationship is all about growth, and two alphas will always be willing to learn.

As I said, not all Alpha men can handle Alpha women, but not all Alpha men are scared to date and marry us, either!

Tired as Hell of Pretending

On Relationships

By Dr. Shekina Farr Moore

It wasn't until much, much later in life that I began to hear this "alpha female" phrase coined. Truthfully, I had no clue what an alpha was nor did I think the chic had any relevance to me. It took me a pretty long time to articulate what made me so peculiar; and then longer than that to then embrace my alpha for two reasons—1) Ignorance. I didn't know how to articulate why I was so different; and 2) I didn't see being an alpha woman as a *good* thing but rather as a thing that pushed people away...especially men!

Ignorance

I mean in school, no one explained personality traits and at home I was always told I had a strong personality. I didn't always see it as a compliment growing up when my mom would say, "You're just like your Daddy!" I didn't come to appreciate this until much later in life. I wanted to be like my mom because everyone liked my mom and gravitated toward her. I seemed to have the opposite affect. Even when I was "nice", I didn't evoke the same likability. I'm going to keep it real with you because this is will make you tired. Listen. Sis was tired.

Thank God for my mom. I remember being picked on for being bossy and constantly told that I was "on my high horse". As a kid I didn't know how to turn off my personality. I just knew that I was rubbing people the wrong way just by being myself. I was praised for getting things done, for being efficient and for taking charge when it benefitted my friends but quite the opposite when my energy occupied a room.

Literally, to this day, when I walk into a room all eyes are on me. I kid you not. And it's not just beauty, it's presence; it's a je ne sais quoi. It's what my mom prepped me for all those years while I didn't quite yet understand.

She would say, "One day you're going to appreciate that gift of boldness."; "God is going to use you to do great exploits with that attention-commanding presence of yours";

"You're unique, even your name commands awe." I mean, my mom was and is THE TRUTH! A consummate edifier, she knew I was an Alpha and reminded me daily who I was and to embrace my Alpha.

I was completely ignorant to the power I yielded. I used to think that boys just thought I was attractive physically but I now know they saw something primal—a potential "worthy" make that could help them build a Kingdom. But mama knew.

Did you know? When women come from a strong, solid family foundation, they feel they have more courage to venture out. A motherly female role model (whether the mother was alpha or not) also gives encouragement to a budding alpha personality.

I didn't see being an alpha woman as a good thing

While in college I can't tell you how many times I dated a guy who tried to dampen my fire and dim my light. I thought I had to play small and flicker my flame in order to be accepted. I let a man put his hands on me, give me a black eye and another choke me out. Who had I become? Why was I so broken and lost?

I was raised to embrace by fiery and bold personality. Yet here I was allowing a man who made scenes in 5 star restaurants to treat me like a servant. Hell, no. I was tried as hell of pretending to be less than I knew I was. I was tired as hell of hiding my dreams and holding back the answers to questions that puzzled him. I was tired as hell of not being able to identify with someone that I thought was pretty damn amazing. I was tired of being Ms. Goody-Two-Shoes and pleasing everybody but my damn self. I needed to say it *just like that*.

While being an alpha female is incredibly powerful, alpha females also report some negative aspects. The research participants in a study in the *Journal of Leadership Education* expressed having to pay a price for their status and strong alpha female identity.

They felt at times that they were negatively labeled and stereotyped. They also reported feeling forced to live up to very high expectations.

After being choked out in college at the hands of a man I was dating, I took a hard look at myself and the concessions I was making to accommodate others, to put others at ease with my bright they constantly wanted to dim. From that ordeal arose a *fierce* woman.

I'm Trudie's Granddaughter

On Relationships

By Aisha N. Martin

My grandma Trudie, God rest her soul, raised 13 children on her own, six boys and seven girls. THIRTEEN!! She was one of the strongest women I know. She put the *A* in Alpha Female! She empowered her sons AND daughters the same way. She equipped them with the tools they needed to be self-sufficient.

She was resilient, classy, outgoing, wise, nurturing and caring. She stressed the importance of education, finances (even though she was far from "rich") and most importantly operating in boldness and using your voice.

She was a 4'11" powerhouse who said what she meant and meant what she said, "*and though she is but little she is fierce*!" She loved telling people the story about the time my cousin Tiki and I were riding with her in the car and as much as we loved each other and couldn't stand to be separated, we wouldn't stop arguing.

She pulled over on the side of the road, laid down the law as only an alpha female could and in her words "*after that, you could've heard a rat piss on cotton.*" Ha, ha man I miss that woman (sigh).

The alpha-ness in my mother is a direct result of my grandmother hence the reason I think I was born into this world an alpha female. No, seriously. Instead of falling into the A, B, O blood groups, I think my blood type is alpha! (Lol) My mother is no-nonsense because her mother was no-nonsense and you guessed correctly, I don't entertain foolishness either.

Research has shown that alpha females have extremely high emotional intelligence. Emotional intelligence (aka EQ or EI) a term created by two researchers – Peter Salavoy and John Mayer is our ability to recognize, understand and manage our own emotions and recognize, understand and influence the emotions of others.

So, when would an alpha female need to manage her emotional intelligence? According to Salavoy and Mayer, it's when:

- **Giving and receiving feedback**
- **Meeting tight deadlines**
- **Dealing with challenging relationships**
- **Not having enough resources**
- **Dealing with change**
- **Dealing with setbacks and failure**

When it comes to relationships, as an alpha woman I have had to learn to pick my battles and let someone else take the lead. Let me tell you, this is no easy feat. I'm still a work in progress, trust me. I told you earlier that Trudie, the ultimate alpha woman raised my alpha mom who then raised me. So, believe me when I say it's deeply rooted.

"She's also unlikely to hold a grudge, so when you two quarrel, you can resolve issues there and then and move on, as she's not the type to keep rehashing old ugliness forever just for the sake of drama. Once it's over, it's over."

Alpha women have zero tolerance for drama which means we have no time for "drama kings or drama queens for that matter." Emotional roller coasters, passive-aggressiveness, and mind games are immediate turn-offs. Who has time for that? I am a communicator and an effective one if I do say so myself.

So, I have no problem expressing myself when trying to resolve a conflict. I find it very hard not to get perturbed when it takes forever and a day to get your point across because you're repeating the same thing over and over again without addressing the matter at hand.

I also hate it when the vault is opened and old issues are rehashed when I thought it was resolved. I'm like an elephant, my memory is long. The bible says to forgive seventy times seven, but it doesn't say that I have to forget (Hey! I didn't write it). So, just because I don't speak on it, doesn't mean that I've forgotten. I just choose not to dwell on it and hold a grudge. I refuse to let drama consume my life. When I'm done, I'm done.

"Alpha women value and appreciate integrity...If you need her, she's there for you. If she makes a promise, she will keep it unless she's incapacitated."

Many people observe alpha women conducting business and assume that we're cold-hearted, brazen, arrogant and selfish. That couldn't be further from the truth. We are very passionate about the things that we love and those we love. We are nurturing and very loyal. If I have it, you have it.

If you need me, I have your back and I will be there. I will ride for you until the wheels fall off. I find it very hard to ask someone to do something for me, but if I do or if help is offered and I'm told that it will be done that's what I expect to happen. I expect the same love and respect that I give.

The loyalty that alpha women possess makes it hard for us to tolerate excuses or broken promises. My word is my bond and my name means something. Aisha means life in the Swahili language. When people speak my name, I want it to be said that I lived my best life and one that was authentic and one that was filled with integrity.

"If you've always dreamed of being the knight in shining armor to a damsel in distress, that's not what you're going to find in this partnership."

In previous relationships and even in marriage I've had to bite my tongue, woosah and have my very own private girl chat and decide if it's really worth it for me to get a migraine. I'm an analytical problem solver, so I strategize and come up with solutions. I don't bring my problems to the table without a plan A, plan B and in some cases a plan C. I don't add more fuel to the fire then sit back and wait for someone else to extinguish it.

Therefore, when I'm presented with problem after problem, complaint after complaint with no solution and no plan in sight it tap dances on my last nerve. That's when my alpha gene kicks into gear and I just say, I got this. I'll handle it. Don't even worry about it; I'll take care of it.

However, marriage is supposed to be a partnership. I didn't get married in hopes that my husband would complete me. I was already whole I needed a partner. I needed someone with vision and goals that complimented mine and someone who was ready to take over the world together. Men by nature are hunters and protectors.

I am very independent and will never act like a damsel in distress, but through maturation what I've learned over the years is that no man wants to feel like he's not needed. A man wants to feel like he's a **necessity** and not just an **accessory**.

I am learning how to let go and let God. If the decision that's made isn't the one that I would've chosen and even if I feel or KNOW I can do it better, I'm learning to co-pilot and let my husband handle situations and put out fires.

This doesn't mean that I don't have a contingency plan. It just means that I am going to let him try to be the man that God has called him to be and I'm going to respect him as the head of our household.

   "You realize that she's with you because she wants to be with you, and not because she needs to be, right? You may have some insecurities about being with such a powerful creature, but guess what? She chose you. She doesn't NEED you."

In the past, even though the words never came out of my mouth I had the mindset and attitude of "I want(ed) you, but I don't NEED you." I never had to say it, it showed in my attitude, my walk and let's just be honest my facial expressions tell everything. I've been told on more than one occasion that my eyes speak volumes (ha ha!).

I have no problem being alone. Matter of fact, I really enjoy solitude. It's my time to reflect, relax, "wild out" if necessary and rejuvenate. Boys night out does not bother me. Please, go do your thing, because I love a good girls' night out.

I have never been that female that HAD to have a boyfriend 365 days/year because I couldn't be alone or had to always be creased up under someone. I can do bad all by myself, so I refuse to hold onto someone and stay in a relationship just for the sake of having one. I have been in relationships where I've been followed even though I was going out with his sister!

I've been questioned about where I'm going and how long I planned to be there, in a manner that felt more like an interrogation. I'm Trudie's granddaughter so you know that didn't end well. My phone has been searched and my emails have been read. This level of insecurity is incomprehensible to an alpha female.

Know this, if we're together that means that I chose YOU. You don't ever have to question that. I could be with anybody. I could be single. I remember like it was yesterday, I was in college and dated 2 guys at different times and both cheated on me. One was hiding phone numbers in a *Planters* Cheez Balls can which was dumb because that was a snack I loved at the time and even in his "pimped out" Tracker SUV that I loved driving.

I mean, there were numbers tucked into the seat belt which rained down on me when I put it on. Numbers in the visor, numbers in the glove compartment. For a man in the military, he had a lot of time on his hands. The other, well let's just say he was something else. You can imagine in both situations I was furious and offended because after all, I chose THEM remember?! Clearly, they didn't really know who they were dealing with or how this thing works.

I'm Trudie's granddaughter, so I can show you better than I can tell you. My peace of mind is valuable and time is precious. Time is something you can't get back, so I refuse to waste mine. So, in the words of Beyoncé, all of their things were in a box to the left, to the left. However, they were both immediately remorseful and tried coming back.

Men like this always do when they're with an alpha woman. Alpha females know their worth, so we don't compromise and accept anything less than that. So, when you've been with an alpha woman you know what you've lost. One showed up at my door looking like he hadn't slept or eaten in days and the other was acting as a DJ leaving his favorite playlist on my answering machine every day for two weeks.

Alpha females are the best women to date and definitely the one you want to make your wife. We're adventurous and are usually the life of the party which means the relationship will never be boring. We're ambitious, so you will definitely need to match our hustle otherwise you'll feel as if you got left at the train station.

We have high standards and goals, so we will always challenge our partner. We turn heads because we just have a natural glow. We stand out in a crowded room. We make an entrance without even trying. There's just something about us that people can't put their finger on. They're drawn to us and don't know why.

"SHE'LL ALWAYS BE 100% UPFRONT WITH WHO SHE IS. You never have to guess if she's putting on a front just to reel

you in because she doesn't really care what you think. She'll be her authentic self because she lives by the mantra, "Take me as I am, or watch me as I go." She holds her dignity in high regard and doesn't feel the need to act innocent and fragile just to avoid scaring you off."

We are very confident in who we are and don't seek validation. For some that is attractive and for others who can't handle that level of confidence it's intimidating. We don't play games! We are very direct and intentional in our speech. We don't sugarcoat what we say, so there's no room for confusion. You will have no problem understanding what we meant. We're very clear. Our yes means yes and our no means no. There's no grey area. If you're in a relationship with an alpha female or contemplating being in one, cherish her, respect her and don't let her go. If you don't, she'll be hard-pressed to stick around because when we're done it's a wrap. Know that she chose you and she did so for a reason, so don't question her love and loyalty to you. We are ride or dies unless you make us choose otherwise.

Don't slack in your ambitions unless you want your alpha female to lose interest and make plans without you. An alpha woman seeks a partner, so if she sees that in you don't take it for granted. She's loyal, so if she says she's got you then she's got you!

It may not always be easy and you may have to work for it, but good things usually don't come easy. However, trust me when I say that deciding to take a chance on an alpha woman will be the best decision you've ever made.

Still not convinced?

Well, I'm Trudie's granddaughter, so I can show you better than I can tell you.

Don't Believe Me Just Watch

On Careers

By Aisha N. Martin

"I'm a very strategic thinker and planner and so I always laugh when people ask well how did you figure out how to be the First Lady? And I'm like well; I went to Princeton, Harvard. I was a corporate attorney. I worked for the city. I ran a non-profit organization. I was the Senior Vice-President. I mean that's what happens to spouses sometimes is that all of that, it's wiped away. It's sort of almost like, so you're shocked that I can do this job?! Ok, alright but that's something to remember because that part of me disappeared ya know. It disappeared over the course of the campaign. It was almost like my whole history. I became Michelle Obama. I became Barack Obama's wife. I became the First Lady and again you can fight against that or just kinda go ok, alright, I get it, I get it… alright. So, you're not sure whether I can do this. Um, ok, well, let me show you."

When my forever First Lady, as I affectionately like to call her, uttered those words on BET's *A Thousand Words with Michelle Obama,* a smile and sense of pride swept over me. I chuckled, clapped and screamed at the TV "You tell 'em First

Lady!" Hey, don't judge me. I was having an alpha woman bonding moment. All I could do was shake my head in agreement and reflect on how many times people have doubted my abilities to deliver, and I would think to myself, ok alright, I get it, I get it alright. Despite my degrees, my resume that lists all of my qualifications, you don't think I can do THIS job?! Ok, well let me show you!

Science of the People's article entitled *The Alpha Female: 9 Ways You Can Tell Who is an Alpha Woman* defined an Alpha woman as **a woman who has embraced her leadership ambitions. She is talented, highly motivated, and self-confident**.

Their research, found that Female alphas embrace their confidence which helps them lead others and tend to:
• **Believe her ability to achieve is limitless**
• **Self-identify as an alpha female**
• **Have a confidence that is contagious, which leads others to respect her as an equal**
• **Showcase leadership characteristics**
• **Be recognized by others as being impactful**
• **Have extremely high ambitions**

As a Scientist what I found most interesting in the article was that the term 'alpha' actually comes from research on animal behavior and ironically females rarely lead the pack in the animal kingdom.

Dr. Jennifer Smith, a Biologist at Mills College in California and her colleagues conducted a study into female leadership among mammals and found that of the 76 non-human mammal species that exhibit leadership, only seven have females that take charge during conflict, foraging or travel.

Of these seven species, females fit a certain definition of leadership. Smith and her team found that these females possess one or more of the following traits: they are physically stronger than males, they are long-lived or spend most of their life in one area, and they form strong social bonds with other females.

According to Smith, "in these species, females are bonded to each other, and they influence their society's structure through directing food collection, fighting wars, deciding where their group moves and holding local knowledge useful for finding food." Wow! How awesome is it to be so confident in your abilities, leadership skills and the power you hold that the presence of another female poses no threat to you, therefore you have the innate ability to forge authentic intentional relationships with them.

Remember this. Confidence is contagious and "real recognizes real."

"Because alpha females have such high emotional intelligence, they often serve as social lubricators and business mediators. Alpha females often are able to bring social ease to a group. They tell jokes. They start conversations. They introduce people. They smooth over business disagreements and take charge."

In the 2015 study *Leadership Influences of the Veteran Alpha Female Leader* conducted by Danielle J. Moncrief, she found that the majority of the female leaders she interviewed referenced the ways their racial, ethnic, or minority experiences influenced their motivation. Many participants seemed to use this influence of motivation as a catalyst for their achievements in leadership.

The veteran alpha leaders discussed how particular challenges motivated their desire for social change, awareness workplace bias, or drive for success. Psychotherapist and international bestselling mental strength author Amy Morin believes that by adopting some of the strategies men use to advance their careers women could help level the playing field in male-dominated industries.

Morin believes that by challenging traditional gender roles women who exhibited stereotypical "masculine traits" such as aggressiveness and confidence received 1.5 more promotions than men who exhibited similar qualities.

According to Morin, women should be assertive communicators. A 2014 study published in *Harvard Business Review* found that women are often silent in meetings compared to men, but when they did they offered apologies and allowed themselves to be interrupted. Let's just say this alpha female doesn't have that problem...EVER! I have never struggled to communicate and make my voice heard nor do I tolerate disrespect. We may not agree, but my ideas will be heard, and you can't just dismiss me.

Alpha women know what they want and they're unapologetic about it. They know how to articulate it and they know how to get it. Does this resonate with you? Then STOP APOLOGIZING!

Alpha women are social butterflies, problem solvers, leaders, social activists, entertainers. We bring about change. We make things happen! I am often called upon as a mediator because I'm good at finding common ground and resolutions. When I worked for an airline in their First Class lounge I was nicknamed "Oprah" because passengers were known to grab a drink, sit at my desk and tell me all of their problems and life stories up until it was time to board their flight.

That's not uncommon for an alpha woman, because people are naturally drawn to us like a moth to a flame. That's not my ego talking, it's fact. We shine without even trying and it's attractive, intriguing. People can't put their finger on it, but they know we're different. I'm known to ease tensions, calm nerves and bring a bit of joy into sad situations by cracking a joke, singing a song or dancing to a dope beat.

I never feel awkward in social situations, because no matter where I go I feel that I belong. I always feel that the party doesn't start until I get there (ha ha)!

Accept Credit For Your Work

Morin also found that many women struggle to take credit for their work. As an alpha woman, one thing that I'm protective of is my intellectual property. Knowledge is something that no one can take from you. If I create, edit, revise or implement something my name is always going to be on that document.

I remember like it was yesterday when my supervisor asked me to create several Standard Operating Procedures (SOPs) for our lab. However, he wanted me to leave my name off each document. Each time I presented an SOP to him, he'd return it and ask me to remove my name, and I'd send it right back to him the same way. There was no way that his name was going to remain on my intellectual property and my very existence be erased. Nope! Not happening!

The Struggle Is Real

"While there's no denying that the struggle is real—studies consistently show women leaders experience bias—hosting a pity party won't help. Every minute you spend making excuses is precious time that could have been spent advancing your career. Stay focused on solutions and keep working hard to reach your greatest potential."

A common theme among veteran alpha female leaders in Danielle J. Moncrief's study was the importance of continuous learning. One-hundred percent of those leaders involved expressed appreciation for their ability to learn to face challenges, learn from experience, or learn from others. Many found that their challenges were actually instrumental toward shaping their experience and talents. Alpha females are leaders who:

• **Constantly read books about what they do AND in subjects completely new to them.**
 • **Dive deep into their expertise. They like to be experts.**
 • **Learn about new fields, research, and topics.**
 • **Take professional development courses to further their development.**
 • **Ask questions.**
 • **Learn from their experiences.**

As an alpha female in STEM I am often the only woman in the room and many times the only woman of colour which presents its own set of challenges. I have had to learn how to navigate through workplace bias and attempts to dismiss me, embrace challenges because they've helped strengthen me and not lose my identity or voice in the process.

While many of these challenges have come from men, sadly most have come from other women who felt threatened by my presence. So much in fact that, I have been on the receiving end of spiteful, malicious attacks on my character and work performance.

Alpha women are leaders, boss ladies who are not easily **intimidated**, but often seen as **intimidating**. While employed in the lab at a certain government agency that shall remain nameless, one female co-worker went as far as to contaminate my clinical samples, AND the reagents I used to process those samples. In the end what I realized is that while I was in the mindset of learning from seasoned Scientists including her, expanding my skill set and strengthening my resume she felt threatened and was trying to dull my shine.

However, one thing I'm certain of is that I am divinely and uniquely made, so there's no one like me. "I have never had to unscrew another woman's light bulb in order to shine." It's unfortunate that she felt the need to do so. I am often imitated, but never duplicated because I am authentically and unapologetically me and that's my superpower.

I am an analytical problem solver, so things such as constant complaints, excuses, and problem after problem with no solution really irk my alpha spirit.

Don't get me wrong I've had some bumps along the way in my journey both personally and professionally. However, I'm not down for long, and I don't waste time complaining about what happened. I dust myself off, analyze the situation, and I get back up again stronger, better than before and definitely a lot wiser!

A supervisor (a female if you can believe that) once told me that I'd never make it as a Scientist. She said that I was nice, a team player and very organized so I should consider being an administrative assistant. She clearly didn't know who she was talking to, or the magnitude of the effect that her words would have on me.

I've accomplished a lot of things and you think I can't do THIS job?! My mission from that day forward was to prove her wrong. Me?! Fail? Failure is not an option for an alpha woman. We can't stand when someone tells us what we're not capable of doing. That's like vibranium to us.

My last words to her were, ma'am you're entitled to your opinion, but you don't know me very well or what I'm capable of. You may see my name in print, or you may see me in person, but trust me you WILL see me again. Guess who she saw a year later in a different lab department performing at a high level as a SCIENTIST? You guessed correctly, me! My name has been in print more than a dozen times, so I've fulfilled that promise as well. Do you think I should send her a signed copy of one of my books (wink)?

"Throw me to the wolves and I will return leading the pack."

Alpha women are often misunderstood and underestimated. So, the next time you encounter an alpha woman, take the time to get to know her. She will be the best friend that you've ever had because she's loyal and supportive.

She will take your business or idea to the next level because she's innovative. She will close that deal, because she's confident, articulate and outspoken. She doesn't back down from a challenge. She will elevate your event with her professionalism and perfectionism.

She will be your right hand, your subject matter expert because of her expertise; because she's well read. She's a leader who will bring order to chaos. She's the one people will be fighting to collaborate with. Ask me how I know. Because I'm that ALPHA WOMAN.

Don't believe me? Just watch….

Making *Her*

The Evolution of the Alpha Woman

By Dr. Barbara L. Swinney

Growing up the youngest of ten (six girls and five boys) was like having my own little entourage to support me and cheer me on. From the very beginning—the very moment they learned that mama was pregnant they fought over me.

The boys wanted another boy so that they could expand their Kingdom and the girls wanted another girl so that they could maintain their Queendom. I can remember times when my brothers and sisters would literally have physical fights over taking me, THE BABY, on a trip to a friend's house or showing me off to that someone special. My family openly celebrated my every milestone and constantly sent me the "Midas Touch" message. When I started walking, they erupted with praises, *"Yeah...the baby is walking!"* I said my first word, *"Yea...the baby is talking!"*...*Yea, the baby is going to school; the baby is graduating, the baby got her doctorate; the baby got a promotion!* Seeing Barbara do BIG things just became an unspoken norm.

My siblings simply loved me. They fought for me, with me, and sometimes through me. They taught me that I was special—that I mattered. They taught me to love and respect myself; and they were going to be darn well sure that others would do the same.

My brothers protected me and made sure I had everything I needed. They taught me how to swim, how to drive, how to change an alternator on a car, and how to recognize a knuckle headed boy. My five sisters provided the guidance and cultivated my gifts to inspire and see far beyond the world around me.

They sparked my interest in reading, taught me how to chronicle my feelings in a journal, and how to tell somebody off without saying a word. They taught me how to persuade as they put me up to butter up our parents to get something they wanted. They knew that I was good at presenting a powerful case and moving people to work together for a greater good; good being whatever they wanted at the time. Their praise and consistent reassurance reinforced who I was and gave me the confidence to dream—to believe that I could do and be whatever I wanted. My family affirmed me and grew me into a woman who is all things ALPHA!

The Evolution

Go FAR! Dream BIG! Believe BIG! My family made me believe that I could do and be whatever I wanted and I wanted more! I was going to work harder, run farther, and achieve more than I had ever seen
anyone accomplish around me. I was determine to be the picture of success.

I was so determined not to be like her. Mama worked all day as a maid and still attended to Daddy's every need. She would cook his dinner and express deliver it to him as he sat expectantly in his recliner.

Always running around the house picking up after the ten of us—never having time for herself. Yet, Mama seemed so happy leaving our home to go and take care of theirs, the Verdin Family, the family to which she committed more than ten years of her life. She would wake up every morning, literally singing as she sent us off to school. I watched her gladly go to work. Though I never uttered a word to her, I resented the fact that my mother was a maid—The Help.

By the time I came along, most of my friends' parents had office jobs, so I was a bit embarrassed to tell them that my mother was "the help". I just did not understand why she would leave her own house and her own children every day to go and take care of another family; to go and cook and clean for someone else. I would always hear my father tell her that she did not have to go; he could provide for us, but she just had to go.

Mama was a gifted caretaker, but I just did not get it! I love my mother, but I could not see myself waiting on anyone the way that she did. Not me! I would take every opportunity to make my life look differently. Chasing one degree after another…one promotion after another, I simply refused to give into her life. I developed a laser-like focus on building a career. I established myself as a wife, mother, and a career woman. Still, I could not breathe—cloaked by sadness; empty and paralyzed by the realization that I was wrong about Mama…wrong about the idea of success.

I just kept thinking, *"What in the hell is wrong with me...Is this even what I'm supposed to be doing?"* I had achieved everything that I set out to achieve. I had everything that resembled success—a beautiful family, a nice home, a thriving career, a doctoral degree, and what looked to be the makings of an extremely promising future.

So, why did I find myself crying on the floor of my closet; pleading to God to give me my passion back. I cried out to Him and He said NOTHING! Not that night, anyway.
I attended a leaders' conference sponsored by my company. At the close of the session, I was chatting with friends when I felt a tap on my shoulder.

When I turned around, my supervisor and the head of human resources were standing there. Having worked as a supervisor with these people, I was familiar with what happened after the shoulder tap. "Barbara...Can we find a place to talk?" We went into an empty room, where there just "happened" to be a table set with three chairs. Clearly, this was planned. "I'm glad you're sitting down." I thought, "That was stupid." He had just asked me to have a seat. He continued, "Well, we've interviewed quite a few candidates for the director's position (a position below mine) and we just can't find the right fit." I chuckled inside. I had been a part of the interview team for every single interview—he was never in the room, but OK, proceed.

He went on to say that, they felt that I had a unique skill set and they needed me to go and turn the division around. My supervisor and I had been at odds since he had joined the team. He just did not understand the big picture or valued my gifts as a visionary leader and had made a point, on several occasions, to remind me that I was his subordinate.

I can remember being in meetings, he would pose a question and I would have the soundest response in the room (my team members would even defer to me) and he would literally disregard my answer only to accept the very same answer from someone else. Ignoring me and devaluing me had become his practice. I was sure that this meeting was his doing.

In disbelief, I uttered, "So…are you telling me that I'm being demoted?" Neither offered a reasonable response. I had seen this strategy before. I felt sick to my stomach! I had never faced a challenge in my career. Everything I

had worked for—unmatched results and an exemplary record of accomplishments—tarnished. The mosaic of my identity, meshed by my role as a wife, mother, and a leader in my field; suddenly unidentifiable.
Darn it! There it was again; that sadness that I had experienced earlier.

This was my "why am I here" moment. I started to examine my life. Grappling with the questions: What is it all for? Why am I here on this earth? Just what was I sent here to do? These questions led me back to the trail of tears on my closet floor and pointed me directly to my mother's life; the life that I did not want. I had given everything for to create the life I wanted.

What do you do when you have given everything for the life you wanted and the life you wanted does not give anything back to you? I did not just want to be "among the living"; I wanted to feel what it really meant to live.

I was so determined not to live my mother's life—a life that I did not want. How ironic was it that I still ended up with a life that I did not want. Suddenly, things were so different. Far outside of what I had planned and nothing like I had hoped. I was angry, disappointed, and broken hearted, but in the light of my ALPHA, I was not just going to sit there and quietly allow life to slap me in the face. I had to figure this out…I had to figure ME out.

Just how was the shift in my career connected to the looming sadness that I continued to experience? This was the catalyst for the evolution of this ALPHA Woman!

The Real ALPHA Woman

I had the painful realization that I did to my mother the same thing that was done to me—I devalued her gifts and misconstrued her tenacity. I did not see the big picture. I discounted her ALPHA.

In looking at my mother's life more closely, I realized that Mama, like a true ALPHA Woman, served in the way that she did because she understood that her purpose was outside of herself. She recognized that she was sent to this earth to use her gift of nurturing to be of service to others.

Mama was not THE help; she knew that she was sent here TO help. She knew exactly how helping looked, set her sights on it, and refused to stop until she fulfilled her "why".

I decided to go and introduce myself to the new staff. From the moment, I started speaking, sharing my story and encouraging them to tell theirs, they hung on every word. I could tell that they were moved by what I was saying. I remember thinking, "These people are counting on me. Barbara, this is not about you! It's so much bigger!"

Getting the tap on the shoulder that day, was God's response to my "in the closet" plea for passion. It was not that I had lost my passion; God was repositioning for purpose. No longer chasing after things with waning value; things that will not matter after I leave this earth. In true ALPHA Woman fashion, these days, I am hawking down purpose!

The Alpha Woman Reactivated

Finding My Alpha Again

By Dr. Barbara L. Swinney

"Which one of y'all just kicked me?"

I felt like Chris Tucker in the movie, *Rush Hour!* My life was living a life of its own—turning back flips and popping wheelies, with me holding on with a death grip. I just did not understand what was happening to my life or whose life I was living. Clearly, I was not in control.

Just two short months after receiving that tap on the shoulder from my supervisor and the head of human resources and the consequent reassignment to a lesser role, I discovered that I was a supporting actress in a marriage that, I am sure, was made for a Lifetime® Movie.

I had not had the time nor the space to wrap my mind around the major shifts that were occurring in my career when I discovered that my husband was engaged in a long-term affair. The two things, my marriage and my career, that most readily defined me, looked nothing like I had imagined. This was just too much to deal with all at once. I figured that if I was going to get out of this pit, I had better start climbing. Since my marriage affected the most people, I thought I should start there.

Dazed and confused, I made my way to my therapist's office. I had so much in my head. Everything I thought I would say, I did not. I anxiously waited to meet with my counselor to discuss the demise of my marriage. I had my tears on ready and my anger set to trigger; just waiting to let her eavesdrop on the conversation in my head; the inner banter about how I found out that my husband was living a double life for years and within thirty days of our divorce, he was engaged.

The selfishness, arrogance, and recklessness of the two of them—chronicling their affair by posting pictures on social media with no regard or respect for our children or our respective families. How was I supposed to help my girls navigate this dysfunction? The pain and agony of realizing that the last twenty years of my life was an illusion, of sorts, was bewildering. The man that my girls and I greeted at the door upon his return from his "business trips", was really returning to us from his other life—one in which we did not exist. In this house of cards, she was the "wife". Who does this? The depth of the deception was mindboggling and left me questioning my identity, my judgement…my intelligence.

Reassuring myself, I continued to engage in my internal dialogue, "I know I am smart; brilliant in fact. I am a good woman. Any man would love to be my partner in life. How did I miss this? Why did I allow myself to accept so little from him?"

As I sat there, I began to wallow in my anger, disappointment, and disillusionment. The longer I sat in my puddle of self-pity, more and more people made my angry list. I blamed my family for cultivating an insatiable appetite for something, someone outside of myself to validate me; they had always affirmed me.

In this moment, I felt like their adoration and praise had the adverse effect. None of them told me that the world was not as kind as they were. I blamed my friends who constantly looked for me to have it all together; and I blamed myself for meeting their expectations.

I wanted to go to each of them and scream, "You were wrong…you taught me wrong…you treated me wrong…you ruined me!" I felt like I was living everyone else's truth.

Finally, the counselor entered the office and crashed my pity party. We exchanged pleasantries and then it was time, time for me to let her in on my diatribe! I opened my mouth, ready to spew it all, and nothing! None of the thoughts would form into words. In the very moment that I attempted to speak, I had a stunning revelation.

Almost every sentence or question I posed during my mental babbling included the word "I" (How did "I" miss this? "I" allowed… "I" lost...). It became clear that "I" was in the middle of it all. My anger and urge to blame dissipated and I became less interested in hating my ex and more concerned about my healing. If I were going to truly, *live* the rest of my life, I would have to get to me again.

I would have to reconnect with myself— find my ALPHA and take the steps necessary to mend my broken heart.

Standing in My ALPHA

This was a time to remember who I was. I had to remember the little girl who was doted on by her family. I had to remember that I was, indeed, special. I had to remember the gifts that my family had cultivated in me long ago. I had to remember that I was a woman who deserved true love and respect; a woman who knew what she wanted and had the confidence to go and get it.

I had to remember that I was an ALPHA Woman…and baby…she is BACK!
I started with taking 100% responsibility for my current reality. Nothing that happened to me was my fault, but it was certainly my responsibility. I accepted less that I deserved; I ignored the signs of emotional abandonment, abuse, and infidelity; I did not hold my husband accountable, and I stayed far longer than morally obligated.

My behavior was not aligned with what I had envisioned for my life, but I made no adjustments (other than hope and pray that he would change). In accepting responsibility, I was able to determine a path forward.

I also had to regain custody of myself.
I had surrendered so much of my power and personal control to my husband …to the marriage. I lost sight of who I was as an

individual, how to make decisions for myself, and simply how to run my own life. A prime example of this was blindly allowing my husband to handle all the finances. I did not engage in this process, so when I found myself having to manage it all, I would literally have panic attacks.

These were times when I had to take deep breathes and remind myself that I was smart, capable, and had the capacity to build a sound financial foundation for my girls and me. With God's grace, and some professional help, I have been amazed at the financial powerhouse that has emerged! I had to take charge of every aspect of my life. After I got my footing, it was now time for me to stand—time to stand in my ALPHA.

This would prove to be most difficult, as it would require me to forgive. I had to find a way to forgive myself and everybody involved. I had to make a decision. I could walk around for the rest of my life considering my failures as a wife and despising my ex and his girlfriend for their duplicity, or I could release all of us and grow into the greatness that had been suppressed by the toxic relationship.
Through the process of forgiveness, I have learned to empathize and

have compassion for others. I have learned that people, generally, are not demonstrating destructive behavior from their bad places; instead, they are acting from the places where they are wounded.

In the very essence of the ALPHA Woman, I share my story to help others. I have found many women just like me on this path. Many of them who do not have the emotional tools or resources to deal with grief in a way that is productive. Seeing themselves reflected in my story brings them hope; seeing myself in them, gives me peace.

It does not match what I had in mind; my life…my family looks completely different today. There are far more people involved who, like it or not, have influence in the lives of my girls and continue to impact my life in some way. I cannot stay there.

This simply means that this ALPHA Woman has to continue the practice of taking responsibility for my own behavior—my life, maintain custody of myself, continue to use my story to help others heal, and forgive quickly…over, and over again.

Healthy Relationship or Dominance?

Can the Alpha Woman Have Both?

By Dr. Koyah Alston

"We are Alpha Women. We transcend the fiery darts of life with the ferocity of the Phoenix, escaping the fire we fiercely fly-fierce, freely focused, and unafraid."

"Are you an alpha woman," he said?

There's the question...That which begins to define the way that this will go. Do I A.) play it coy and pretend that I'm just like everyone else and not super alpha? B.) pretend to be a complete damsel in distress (though) I don't quite know how to be that which I totally am not and probably would do a horrible job at faking the funk as a less than strong character or *C.)* come clean, tell him who I am and see if he's strong enough, confident enough, and secure enough to handle it?

So many times, potential suitors say, "You have it all…have it all together. I don't know what I could add?" As I lay in bed solo on sizzling Saturday nights praying for the day to come where the one strong enough to lead the leader in me to find me, I am swept up with ferocious frustration. I am like a calculated spider caught in a widened web that relentlessly traps me as victim, though I am a natural-born victor.

This continual wandering web in my relationship life as an alpha woman paints me as a casualty of love's torrid terrain. I feel as if a negative character in some deplorable place far from fantasy forever flourishing. Thus, I-the alpha woman-sometimes feel demonized, because I am certainly all ardently-alpha-strong topped off with a huge, humongous scoop of a cleverly controlling nature.

Controlling- who me? "You have to always be in control and always want to run things," the men I've dated have often strongly asserted. Controlling—a word no one wants to own. However, for me, there is no denying that my "alphaness" causes me to attempt to control every minute of every day. It's a must that I plan out a witty, well-thought-out execution that leads daily to an accumulation of mountain-sized wins and positive progressions that has to transpire for me every day of existence.

I recall a time in my doctoral program in Leadership Studies when we were given the opportunity to take a personality inventory assessment. Out of all my colleagues in the room, I was noted to be off the scales in the controlling personality type. At the same time, I was also shown to be one of the most empathetic, which amazingly softened my harder, take charge of things nature.

What did that mean about me, as an alpha female? Yes, I like to be in control, set the agenda, create the plan, make sure that things are moving forward, and everything is executed. Yes indeed, I like to be the one to take the lead. Heck ya-I believe in my abilities to limitlessly achieve in any circumstance with blazing confidence and am a visionary.

I lead-always and everywhere, because almost since birth I've always been asked to be in that leader role. What did my alpha female ways mean for me? As soon as I turned into a divorced, single mom on the dating block as a Dr. Mom woman leading two organizations alongside building a media empire as an accomplished empowerment speaker and writer, the meaning of me dating as an alpha woman became crystal clear.

Inner Alpha Demonization

This intrinsic fear of being demonized by potential suitors (males) for my "stereotypically masculine-like" energy actually started while I was very young. I've been an alpha female all my life! I've dealt with the repercussions of my leader strength all my life. All my life, this has been a constant bombardment to my psyche. Taunts of "the man" being screamed into my ears as I rounded another curve on the track subconsciously haunt me in my sleep every now and then.

At times, when I cut my TWA a little too short and catch a glimpse of myself from the side in my mirror as I glide across the room, I hear those voices from my athletic childhood bellowing out. They called me the most horrid names. Those guys would chant in a song-like fashion "the man", as I'd beat them on the track with my muscles beamingly bulging with each stride every time my coach made me run alongside the boys in practice. It was tough being one of the most athletic chicks in the universe during teen years where judgements transformed into verbal jabs. Those hauntings far outweighed the lingering existence of uttered words. I, the track star, won the war of muscular display at 15 with quads and hamstrings larger than most of the boys.

I can still remember the salaciously sweet feeling of victory after beating the guys in sprint reps time after time, showing them up, making them feel bad. "Tom boy", they would utter. Tom boy became a phrase I detested, and I ran swiftly to pink, frilly dresses, high heels, and anything "stereotypically feminine" to receive solace, safety, comfort, and peace with my "alphaness" and further to persuade everyone I was all girl!

Thus, my collision with the opposite sex as an alpha erupted in a clash from a tender age, where my alpha qualities were boomingly demonized.

However, with age comes wisdom; and I now clearly understand that my strength in stature and physique do not make me "manly". Being firm, strong, and a leader is NOT gender-specific or gender-related at all. Conquering childhood demons is an important part of healthy development. As I've grown into womanhood, I am now firmly planted in a space that fully owns the alpha in me and at the same time still wholeheartedly embraces the femininity that I love to display.

As a woman, I am elated to rock my take them down in the boardroom heels. Parading sexy, sophisticated dresses in my everyday life makes me feel good and sexy as I lead. My issue however has been managing others' perceptions of my strength in stature and personality. Intimidation so often roars out from so many in my presence.

However, I am now incredibly comfortable in my own alpha skin because I am keenly aware of the fact that though my presence of mind, body, and spirit can be intimidating to many, I will never hide my shine, dull my light, or temper my strength to make those around me feel more comfortable. I must be free in being the alpha me that I am at all times.

And now, staring in the mirror at the 42-years-old, Dr. mom is single and saddened by the realities of dating as an alpha female. I am so saddened by this reality that I'm working on my own unique dating app to create a space for alpha women like me to be matched with men who truly want an alpha woman. There have been days when I questioned- what's wrong with me? Why am I still single after being divorced for 9 years; and why do so many men tell me I'm (a) such a catch, (b) have it all together, (c) am the perfect package, when my package sits still outside yet to be retrieved? "I'm just happy with Jesus," I tell myself, as I gear up for yet another date, yet another string of first conversations that set the tone for the dating episodes to follow....

My drive—It used to invigorate him. "Who is he," you might ask? Let's just say he wasn't my Mr. Right, but was my Mr. Right Now during a juncture in time when I had such dating hopes. I'd tell him my plans of building my media empire and speaking across the world and his eyes would dance in delight as he literally said he got "pumped" up and even turned on a bit when I talked like that.

He said it made me so very attractive to hear me lead my conference calls and go out to be the boss. However, just as seasons change and rainbows fade away—"Mr. Right Now" became "Mr. Not Right". In the end, he questioned my love and commitment for him, because he said I was (1) always on the grind, (2) married to my work, and (3) made him feel he came second. He was right. Thus, the flame flickered fiercely, but did not last.

And, yet again, I sit here on a Saturday night feeling completely wrapped up in my work- my passion. I'm making deals left and right and figuring out ways to expand my television shows for my TV production company into global markets, while making big wins!

However, the landing of the deal and the added accolades that rack up upon my wall of honors do little to warm me on callously cold nights that cause chattering chills. The new project launch does very little to bring waves of welcoming warmth to my heart that yet is longing.

Is this fulfillment- these lonely nights spent at home Saturday after Saturday with a rolodex full of suitor options, yet still alone? In my speeches, I purport ever-so-boldly, "Just do what you love, and you certainly won't work a day in your life. The joy, happiness, and fulfillment that oozes forth from one living in their passion everyday will cause you to not just exist but live."

This passion-infused way of existence should certainly be enough to warm so tenderly even the coldest blanket on a Sunday night. Yet still, I lay cold. And yet and still-I am wonderfully warmed by my delight as I speak and watch faces aglow and lightbulbs flashing as "ah ha moments" comfort by far. However, I never get too close.

They (the audiences) hold dear to my purported and boldly expressed parameters. And yet, I find myself in the center of the crowd, all eyes on me, yet I am the alpha woman-still alone. I am alone when all the lights have dimmed, everyone has gone home, and the cheering crowds are silenced by the reality of another weekend night's entreat.

I am often misunderstood. Most men tell me I don't want a man; and I simply reply to them that, "I want one, but I don't NEED one since I'm not the needy type." I don't need a man to be single and satisfied as the alpha woman me, because I am so happy with the Lord, with my amazing sons, and with my work.

That's what I always say! And perhaps, when one scales back the layers of truth and lurks down deep into the story behind this smile, the transient truth staring back at me bellows a reality so grim that it took me many years to utter it. They were right. After long hauls of me attempting to be right-THEY were right. I really didn't want a man for many years.

As an alpha woman, it was so easy for me to use my work as my prodding pillow in my comforting zone of work, and I didn't want any man to get too close that he could potentially slow down my grind or my climb to the top. "I can't have anyone get in the way of building my media empire, because life is short, we only have one, and I have to seize the day," I would say to myself.

Yet, on the other hand, I THOUGHT I wanted a man in my life, even seethed at the loneliness at times, but at the end of the day I busied myself with my impassioned work and sacrificed true love's entrance into my successfully driven alpha woman life.

Submission.

That dreaded word that causes so many alpha women to cringe brings up another salient area of misunderstanding. Too many men ASSUME that we as alpha women don't want to submit. Many say that we are so strong and love to lead that we don't know how to submit to their manly leadership. I'd have men tell me, "You don't want to submit, because you're used to leading."

Well, the bulletin board inside my head is however flashing. What they do not understand is that after being the female victor fighting battles after waged wars by day, I simply want to reach and repose in deep entreat in my loving man's arms on regular nights and ordinary days that find me at home with my love. I want the man to lead me. I want to listen to him set the agenda and show me the way to tomorrow and forevers in his care. I want him to take charge and plan, execute, and challenge me to win.

However, too often and tirelessly, I find the ball dropped to new leveled lows if I don't become the leader me and lead us. Too many times, I find no plans made if I don't take charge of the agenda's unfolding and find too many soft words spoken with bated breath instead of strong, assertive let's go's and take-charge no's even. Too many times, I'm completely lost in a sea of "yes men" and meek minds mingled that are unable to lead me to my tomorrow!

The Alpha Man I Seek

Countless times over the past few years, I'd say to myself, "where is the alpha man for me?" He is the one I seek. He is the one I yearn to meet. I may have to build my own bridge to meet him in the stillness of all that I yearn for-that one man who does not flinch at my go-getter drive, firm stride and strong handshake. He greets me as the Dr. Mom that I am and stares at me deeply into my eyes, meeting all my strength within this glance. He sees me-really sees me and is unafraid.

No, he doesn't back down and doesn't shy away. He sees my hustle coupled with the aggressive grind and is bombarded by the calendar that incessantly fills with to dos but resents not its alerts. He basks in the beauty of the dance that I do as the alpha woman rhythm moves me through to new ground and growth.

Driven, he keeps pace. Motivated-he meets me time after time again with equalized measures and pleasantries that make me feel warm all over and challenges my core with chords of depth that delight me throughout. He is elated when I win. He is elated to see me climb, as he takes the backpack from my mountain ride gently from my back with the most alpha man glide and sets just the right set of rightly placed words right on time.

The Truth Set Me Free: And Hence He Found Me

Wow, what a predicament I, the Alpha Woman, was in…all the yearning and loneliness that defined my reality has come to an abrupt end. That was then and this is now. That WAS my story and my trajectory was grim in relation to my goal-finding true love with an alpha man as an alpha woman. Well, as seasons change so can the love and relationship stance and situation of the alpha woman.

It's time to add to my story and report a total turn-around! Fasten your seatbelts. We're going for a ride on love's fast-moving train that sometimes sweeps in when we are unaware.

This is an addendum. I have a new alpha woman experience that has totally transformed my life.

On Facebook a month ago, I wrote the words, "One day he shall find me."

I'm happy to report—thank you, Jesus—I have been found. Dr. G found his one and marriage could even be on the horizon!

At the end of the day, I had a realization that it boils down to one key question for me as an alpha woman-did I want a healthy relationship or dominance? Life happens unexpectedly; and savvy alpha women know how to roll with life's punches and quickly react when immediate maneuvers are needed.

For me, that included a change of perspective and a true look in the mirror at myself. Through writing this book, I came to stare at my truth like never before. I had convinced myself that I was happy with just being the successful business woman and achiever. However, deep down, I truly longed for deep, true companionship to compliment the career success I had found.

Though I was going through the motions of dating, I never really let any of the guys I dated in very close and hid behind the wall of my work. One night, while crying into my pillow, my truth spoke to me like an angelic reckoning beaming from above! My praying turned to crying as I knelt on my knees.

The epiphany came like a beaming flash of brilliant light and it hit me that though I was strong, assertive, and powerful as an alpha woman, I had to let someone in and not be so guarded with my heart that I failed to yield and

bend enough to lower my walls of protection.
"What was I protecting", I thought?
I was so keenly bent on empire building that I
was afraid that if I let someone in, they would
stop by grind and hustle and try to prevent me
from reaching my ultimate goal in life, which is
to leave a legacy for my children by doing
something that nobody has ever done before in
my industry.

I wanted to make my mark on the world in a
way that hadn't yet been done by establishing
a media empire with first-of-its-kind
programming catering to the education and
entertainment needs of the next generation.

These show ideas and educational
programming concepts that I had been honing
for the past 7-8 years (while finishing the
doctorate) had become my refuge and first
love. However, I didn't leave myself enough
time to cultivate the other side of success that I
deeply yearned for inside-love.

I didn't realize that I really wanted that. Yet,
instead of cultivating the needed ingredients
and moves to achieve it, I continued pushing
men away by using my work as an excuse as
to why I didn't have time for a date or to truly
be in a relationship.

At the end of the day, my truth is that I felt successful in my career, but personally unfulfilled. Fore, I longed to have a love of my life! With one rising sun after my night of torrential tears, one text changed transfixed my life. I woke up with new vigor and understanding and seized the opportunity to apply the same drive and tenacity that caused me to win in my career life to the cultivation of my love life.

With a sweet text from Dr. G that said, "Good morning, to my future wife," I was finally open to never again putting him on the backburner of my life and telling him that I didn't have time. I in that moment made a decision to go for what I wanted. Just as I had gone for all I ever dreamed of in the business and educational contexts, for the first time in my life I was all in and going for love. I committed. I went all in and found true love!

I am now walking as boldly as ever in my new alpha woman truth. It is possible to have it all. You can have the alpha woman success in the boardrooms of the world and come home to an amazing alpha man who truly is supportive of you in your grind, not intimidated, and feels absolutely no need to compete.

You most certainly can have all of what you seek, but I had to learn that I don't have to be dominant over my man. I choose a healthy relationship over dominance. It's okay for me to let him lead me at home. It's okay to allow myself to be vulnerable, soft, and tired from the grind of the day in his arms.

It's okay to leave leading at the door and be a submissive woman to my man that values a healthy relationship based on mutual respect for the alphaness in us both! We both support each other's grind. We both become each other's cheerleader.

He understands that when I win-he wins! He gets that I must go get it and set high goals while reaching for the stars, because that's who I am. He understands that I was made to be an eagle and I must soar.

Furthermore, as I soar, he knows his role as my alpha man is to be ready to ensure I have all the resources, support, and love to ensure my flight in life is historic, epic, and out-of-this world in our extraordinary journey through life in love!

Thus-I am now an alpha woman in love! I have found my one. I have found that one fabulous alpha man who loves my

"Alphawomaness" and loves me for the Alpha Woman I am. My Alpha Man has come, and boy am I glowing with glee and alpha woman-filled joy! I'm doing the "happy alpha woman dance" all the way to the boardroom these days and it feels oh so nice!

Strive, Survive, and Thrive

African American Alpha Women Leading in Academic Medicine

By Dr. Koyah Alston

As alpha women, the spotlight is always shining ever so brightly on us. Due to the glow of our radiant ways of operation, people notice us. We live with passionate purpose and fully embrace change, as we are trendsetters and seek to introduce the next wave of greatness through our ingenuity. We take calculated risks, are relentless in pursuit of our goals, and are continually learning to develop ourselves so we can make our mark upon the world and leave a legacy!

We're alpha woman and were born to lead, take charge, and make an impact while inspiring followership. We are truly driven by our ambition and that defines us. By definition, the alpha woman is "a woman who reports being a leader, feeling a sense of superiority or dominance over other females, having others seek her guidance, feeling extroverted in social situations, believing that males and females are equal, and feeling driven" (Ward, DiPaolo, & Popson, 2009; Ward, Popson, & DiPalolo, 2010, p.310).

Though there are a high number of alpha women in the U.S. fitting this definition, a grim picture begins to position its art upon the canvas of the American workplace reality. One would think that given all the amazing, fierce, and extraordinary alpha women in America., there would be countless alpha females who have climbed to the top of the career ladder-despite the male-dominated culture in which we live. That is certainly not the case!

According to Ward et al. (2010), "women in prominent leadership positions (i.e., president, chief executive officers [CEOs], etc.) are still rare, only 3% of CEOs in Fortune 500 companies are women" (p. 310). Further, according to a 2018 article by TriplePundit.com, Mazzoni reports that there are only 2 women of color CEOs at fortune 500 companies. Mazzoni (2018) further shares that in 2016 Ursula Burns left Xerox as CEO, before making history as the first and only Black CEO to occupy the top spot at a Fortune 500 company. The low number of alpha woman leaders in positions of authority at top companies across fields is cause for serious concern.

This issue of the underrepresentation of African American women (in particular) in leadership was so much of a concern of mine that I put on my research hat to delve a bit deeper into a field I was closely associated with, from my background as a higher education administrator-academic medicine.

My guiding question in my research study was related to African American leaders' perception of factors that impacted their advancement as leaders at U.S. medical schools. There were 6 African American females in my study. Each one of these profound alpha women were employed as a dean or a chair at an American medical school; and what they had to share with me about being an alpha woman in the field of medicine was eye-opening!

Not only did these powerhouse women have to make it through four years of college. These astonishing alpha women in medicine had to also successfully get into and through medical or graduate school (with the MDs even having to get through residency) before then climbing the ladder to leadership levels in a male-dominated medical workplace. They had to strive, survive, and thrive to make it as alpha women in medicine and their stories are inspiring to the alpha women of the world!

Setting the Context: A History of Alpha Women in Academia and Medicine

Before I share with you what the 6 alpha women leaders in medicine from my study felt were the keys to making their mark as leaders in medicine, let's first set a little context by looking at the terrain of academic medicine in relation to ethnic and gender diversity.

It was not until 1998 that the first African American woman was appointed to a dean position at a U.S. medical school through the ascension of Barbara Ross-Lee at Ohio State University; however, this appointment of a minority woman to a dean position occurred 127 years after the appointment of the first White woman to a dean position at an American medical school through Ann Preston's appointment at the Women's Medical College of Pennsylvania (Woods, Wetle, & Sharkey, 2018).

Dr. Ross-Lee is certainly an African American alpha woman trailblazer in the field of medicine! In an investigation into national trends of academic appointments of alpha women in medicine it's been found that alpha females were grossly underrepresented at higher rungs of the academic ladder at U.S. medical schools. Women accounted for only 15% of chairs, 33% of vice/senior associate deans, and 16% of deans across U.S. medical schools in 2017 (AAMC, 2017; McDaniel, 2017; Yu et al, 2013).

In the field of surgery, the glass ceiling in surgery for alpha women (1994 to 2015) is still alive (Abelson et al., 2016; Epstein, 2017). These researchers "confirmed that women made up less than 10% of all full professors and calculated they would not achieve gender parity until 2136" (p. 37).

Additionally, there is a growing concern that women are barely there across all leadership ranks as senior faculty, chairs, and deans at medical schools in America (Dannels, McLaughlin, & Gleason, 2009).

Researchers strongly assert that there is a strong need to increase the number of women leaders at medical schools across the United States to address this underrepresentation

(Carnes, Bartels, Isaac, Kaatz, & Kolehmainen, 2015).

Thus to create a larger pipeline of alpha women in medicine, more concentrated efforts are needed to help increase the number of women deans and chairs in academic medicine, given there has only been a tiny increase in the number of women chairs and deans at U.S. medical schools during the 10-year period of reporting from 2004 to 2014 (McDaniel, 2017).

Furthermore, "as long as the current gatekeepers to [leadership positions] do not recognize women as competitive candidates for leadership positions, the number of women in leadership will continue to lag behind their male counterparts" (McDaniel, 2017, p. 19).

While astonishing alpha women across racial/ethnic groups attempting to climb the ranks of leadership in academic medicine face tremendous hurdles and challenges, African American women alphas (in particular) are impacted by additional barriers (Wong et al., 2001).

African American women comprised only 2.8% of U.S. medical school faculty members in 2016; they are of the most severely underrepresented groups among medical school faculty members.

One of the major obstacles encountered by women in academic medicine is that they are severely underrepresented in positions of power (Wong et al., 2001). In 2014, there were only 10 African American women chairs and 66 African American male chairs in comparison with 278 White women chairs and 1,888 White male chairs (AAMC, 2016a).

Hence, Wong and colleagues (2001) underscored the need to prioritize increasing the number of minority women in leadership positions at U.S. medical schools, given that they are the most severely underrepresented group among medical school faculty and leaders.

For alpha women in academic medical environments, there are so many personal factors that affect the recruitment and retention of African Americans alpha women which include: (a) having available mentors; (b) their level of resilience, perseverance, determination, and drive; (c) their leadership skills; (d) their ability to manage expectations; (e) being able to keep a healthy work-life balance; (f) their self-concept; (g) avoiding burnout; and (h) truly being able to manage stress (Jackson, 2004). Alpha women in medicine (in particular) must be savvy to manage these things if they truly expect to thrive and leave their mark as fierce alphas (Jackson, 2004).

For underrepresented minority alpha women in faculty roles, they face so many challenges in regard to the balancing act of clinical, teaching, and research time allocations and the level of support they receive, while engaged in clinical activities (Hamilton, 2016). It has been found to be challenging for alpha women in medicine to manage their time with so many competing demands.

Many African American medical school faculty feel overburdened with a myriad of responsibilities and often find themselves unsupported due to few available mentors leading to other issues, when seeking promotion and tenure (Rodríguez et al., 2014). Consequently, underrepresented minority faculty alpha women remain severely underrepresented and rare as principal investigators on training grants and research projects (Rodríguez et al., 2014).

Alpha Women Leaders in Medicine: Sharing Secrets from the Climb

So, now that we understand the tremendous obstacles and challenges facing alpha women in medicine attempting to lead, it's time to share what some of the alpha women in my study shared with me regarding what helped them to surely thrive in a male-dominated workplace.

These driven African American medical school leaders recounted a lot regarding their experiences as alpha women in the workplace and what impacted their desire to be alpha women leaders.

Iris attended an Ivy League school for her undergraduate education and decided to pick a medical school that she thought would be diverse and serve a broad population of patients. This amazing alpha woman came on a scholarship and admits that she didn't have any money outside those resources provided.

She spent the next 22 years in the military where she learned about leadership and support teams and being in an environment where she felt truly valued for her contributions. She admits that none of the rules of the military applied in the civilian world. She credits the military with teaching her how to truly be a leader.

I attribute my interest in leadership to the military. In the military, the expectation is you will be a leader, whether you were leading a platoon, a company, or a brigade, as you move up. The longer you stay in, the more likely you will be in a leadership position, so I felt that was important, very important . . . Race was not as big an issue when I was in the military.

The military is one of the most egalitarian corporations in the country. The military was one of the first places where White people reported to Black people and Latinos. People don't realize it, but there was race and ethnicity equality in the military large before it occurred in any large corporation in the United States. So, that was not the issue.

Gender was an issue in the military. And I was the first woman in many roles that I played during the 22 years of active duty, so that was an area I learned to manage.

Iris has felt that she's had to fight to be where she is and take a lot of slings and arrows to get to where she is, but learned to strive, survive, and thrive despite the bullets and slings that came her way. What keeps her going is her faith and the fact that she's "not doing it for folks," but instead motivated by a personal, faith-based mission that she has to help the next generation.

I have to survive in this environment, so how do I make sure that I can harmonize? You have to have an unwillingness to take no for an answer, and be willing to wear body armor, and not let the slings and arrows of folks around you totally discourage you. Also, make it about somebody other than yourself. When you go into this environment, if it's all about personal advancement and glory, you could very well get disappointed.

You've got to get beyond that. That's not what motivates me. You've got to really get beyond that. You have to say what is my goal here, to get into a fist fight out on the corner with this person or have another objective? Decide what's most important.

What is your legacy? What is it you want to leave here because if you take every insult as if it's a millstone around your neck, you're not going to make any progress.

For Iris, successfully advancing to leadership levels in academic medicine took sheer grit and "being tough enough to stay in the game."

This alpha woman credits her advancement to leadership levels to her faith and the determination, resilience, self-efficacy, and true perseverance she exhibited throughout her career.

Next, I share the story of the next alpha woman leader in medicine that I interviewed for my study—Felicia. Felicia is a 60-year-old African American alpha woman who is the Chair at a private medical school. She holds a M.D. degree and has been in her current position for 4 years. Her first leadership position at a medical school was in the capacity of a Medical Director.

Within 8 months on the job, her ability to lead and problem solve landed her in an interim role as the Interim Division Director. She's benefited greatly from the consultation and support from her husband who has an MBA from an Ivy league school, given his ability to enter into valuable dialogue about management.

Felicia believes that for a leader in the medical environment, confidence and competence go a long way, coupled with a passion for people development. Collectively, this skillset and disposition allowed her to continually climb quickly and gain recognition, board appointments, and visibility as a competent problem solver at each new organization in which she has worked.

When I came to a certain children's health organization 18 years ago, I don't know how it happened. Somehow, I got put on a committee and this one guy who's the leader said I really appreciate some of the things you said and I think you have really good judgement. That was sort of the beginning and all I was doing was being authentic. I felt they didn't have anybody like me because I was the only Black. Again, getting on those committees, getting in those groups, doing the grunt work.

Felicia found herself starting over career-wise in a new city when her husband's job caused her to move. This alpha woman started out just part-time and working one day per week after 3-4 years of being a mommy doing carpool.

However, her leadership skills and ability to solve problems and take initiative was again realized and she found herself quickly being promoted.

I got to the medical school that I'm at now, and I was just working part-time. They were starting a residency program. I said the one thing I'm really interested in doing is teaching residents at a continuity clinic, so the chair said can you help us get this started? The program director was a mess. He didn't know how to organize anything. I came in and organized it. It wasn't a complicated job. So, I got the residency continuity clinic up and running.

That gave me more confidence; and I basically became her confidant person and she didn't know me from Adam. she just gave me the part-time job because I told her that was what I wanted to do. So that came about.

As an alpha woman, Felicia knows her strengths and what she's good at. Thus, at every opportunity, she volunteered, said yes, and found ways to go above and beyond by demonstrating her skillset and that quickly led to leadership success in the academic medical environment.

In my everyday job I was very good at it . . . I feel like I have a very good ability to know what makes someone tick and very quickly pick up their strengths and their weaknesses when I'm placing people within leadership or developing faculty . . . Umh, so, there was competence in that role. Then, that's how you get recognized for anything else. Then, I was confident. One of the things I've learned and I tell people this . . . I enjoy solving problems, so if you enjoy having a problem and realizing that's what you're there to do then you get the chance to figure it out. That's sort of why I think I like leadership positions and why I have been able to repeat this in other places.

Felicia describes herself as matter of fact, to the point, and one that cuts to the chase as a leader. She has a true passion for helping people to develop and matching them with the place that will help them to grow. She truly believes in being authentic, honest, and always lending a hand to help others. These things have served her well in her attempt to climb to leadership levels in academic medicine.

You know, it fit with my own personal mission. It has to fit with me. It's not about the job. It's about does it make and it's nice being in that place. It's not about the money. It's not about that anymore.

You know, I was supposed to retire this year. That's what I thought, but I'm not ready. It's about enjoyment. It's nice to be in that position to enjoy the work you do because I had some difficult times. I had to let a physician go recently. Senior people resign. I've had somebody be in almost a near-fatal accident, so a lot of problems to deal with and you deal with human beings and their problems, but I can do that where I know there's other parts of this job where I see someone developed so that they're able to go to their next position and who said they learned something and got something out of something that we discussed, so that is all important.

With a feeling that she is living out her personal mission is life as a natural leader, as a true alpha woman, Felica is at a place of true leadership satisfaction, where she is proudly and happily developing talent and using her gifts and strengths every day.

Well, I'm good at managing people. I'm good at figuring out what needs to be done and doing sort of the critical needs things, you know getting the low-hanging fruit. Back then, I didn't know it was low-hanging. They now write about it. You sort of, umh, do the things you can do first, get people on board, and so it's just basically management and understanding what drives folks. I think yes, that's helped me to advance more quickly.

And I think it's a no-nonsense kind of I'm going to tell you what it is. I mean I'm very transparent in my approach. And, I actually like people. I think one of the things that helped me to advance more quickly is just basically management and understanding what drives folks. I actually like people. The other part of what I do is people development.

Find the right people for the right role . . . I started my first leadership role at 34. Now, I'm 60, so in those 26 years there's been a lot of learning on my part as to how to be successful in the role.

Consistent with the commonly purported alpha women characteristics, all of the alpha women in my research study exhibited all of the true traits of alpha women. They were all living with purpose, highly ambitious, go-getters, who never let obstacles or challenges stop them by exercising pure grit, determination, and drive and elevated themselves through their sheer love of learning!

Having gleamed much wisdom and understanding from what it took to strive, survive, and thrive as an alpha woman in medicine from the research study that I did, I developed the Alston Model of African American Career Advancement to Leadership in Academic Medicine.

As a researcher, it was very important to me to outline the key traits and characteristics that helped to contribute to these leaders' advancement to the highest levels of leadership achievement in one of the most brutal and most male-dominated fields- medicine. The emerging themes from my study outlined the key characteristics that the women in my study (in particular) had to exhibit to reach success in leadership as alpha women.

The important characteristics that these fierce alpha women in medicine felt they had to utilize to succeed included: utilizing self-efficacy and being resilient, building powerful networks through mentors and sponsors, exercising a race-conscious professionalism that didn't let the realities of racism or discrimination in the workplace stop them but fuel them to come earlier, work harder, and stay longer!

As African American alpha women leaders in medicine, the women in my study further felt no room for error and the need to outwork their non-minority and male counterparts, often facing low expectations of African Americans or women in their academic and medical work environments.

Lastly, all the alpha women leaders in medicine shared many leadership characteristics that led to their success that they coupled with a strong work ethic and their passionate call to service and giving back to others. These are the traits and attributes that it takes for an alpha woman to succeed professionally-including myself.

What I learned from these alpha women leaders in medicine is consistent with that which I find working as an alpha woman in academia. Thanks heavens it's not all an uphill battle for us as alpha women in the workplace, despite the challenging gender-based systematic barriers that may attempt to deprive us of progression.

More often than not, by proving myself and carving out my own lane to shine, I find myself embraced fully by my male counterparts who many times come to respect my alpha woman assertive grace and style and the way I articulate my points with confidence and poise christened with the leadership acumen and background as an alpha female with a PhD in Leadership Studies.

This foundation has allowed me to make a positive and noteworthy difference and true impact within the boardroom walls. Thus, may we as alpha women embrace and support each other authentically, genuinely, and in a supportive truth that elevates the other to higher heights, so that we totally transform the statistics that leave too many of us missing from the helm of top U.S. companies.

May we as alpha women of the world soar forth as the eagles that we are meant to be. It may be possible in an earth terrain where successful grit, resilience, and perseverance to win can surely win within this world in which we live that is beaming with brilliant light and endless possibilities for us alpha women of the world!

God's Will is Done Through Alpha Women

By LaToya Rose

An Alpha Woman is known as tenacious, forthright, and unmovable. An Alpha Woman listens to advice, suggestions, and critical concern yet she knows her position. She is led by ordinances, principles, and one external entity—God.

God made the Alpha Woman and has the only authority to bring her into focus. She possesses the attributes of God- love, peace, faith, kindness, self-control, gentleness, charity, chastity, and long-suffering. It is not that this woman will not adhere to another human being, it is that she is unable to adhere to another human being.

Remember Ruth, Mary, Rebekah, Hannah, and Abigale in the bible? God loved them as they were women of valor who were compassionate, generous, strategic, unshakeable, fearless, and the handy work of God. Once out of the womb, God has a way of molding one into the Alpha role and placing them in situations, environments, and circumstances so he receives glory.

He needs willing vessels on earth to fulfill his will; therefore, the Alpha Woman is designed to be free with a clean slate as her works will be approved by God.

Life is like a box of chocolates. You never know what you are going to get. The bible tells us in Genesis 2:18 "It is not good for man to be alone. I will make a helper suitable for him." Eve was a dynamic woman who has been misunderstood over the years and her actions have been taken out of context by men who attempt to justify the defiance of Adam to God's command not to eat from the Tree of Knowledge to hid their inability, weakness, and cowardice to follow God exclusively.

In all that Adam lacked, Eve possessed as she was crafted by the hands of God. Although an Alpha Woman- Eve, ate of the apple of the tree of knowledge she also stood forth when God called Adam three times. She was not summoned by God yet she still stood forthright to take accountability of her actions which is why her punishment was not as harsh as Adam.

Many Alpha Women who are ambitious, super-driven, and thrive beyond trauma. She does not allow circumstances to cripple her from achieving her goals. Many misperceived her as a loner living on an island of independent illusion. When in fact, an Alpha Woman has the ability and will to walk away from situations that do not serve God, to stand by her values no matter what, and/or to tell it like it is to maintain peace in her space. When attempting to jeopardize the role, characteristics, and position of an Alpha Woman, one will suffer dire consequences from God.

Friendship

The Oxford dictionary defines friendship as "the emotion or conduct of friends; the state of being friends." Friend is defined as "a person whom one knows and with whom one has a bond of mutual affection, typically exclusive of sexual or family relations." It is an honor to be the friend of an Alpha Woman as this intricate woman brings some great qualities to a friendship.

Although an Alpha Woman is considered strong, firm, and intelligent she stills desires to have genuine concern for her womanhood. There are many people who burden these women with their issues yet are not equipped to aid her in during her times of need. It takes a special person or small circle of people to maintain a healthy friendship with an Alpha Woman.

Every Alpha Woman has that one friend who has been tried and true since day one. This friend not only sees your potential and listen to your sorrows but is equipped to support you beyond struggles, trauma, and moments of limited belief systems.

In 2008 after moving to the east coast from Oklahoma, I found myself in a state of shock and self-discovery. I was a recent college graduate living in a new state where literally no one knew my name, accomplishments, nor passions. During this time, I was working as an assistant manager in retail yet I was internally battling with feeling like I was just going through the motions of adulthood.

While working at my job, a few ladies would frequent often and began to have meaningful conversations with me. We found out we had our sorority, education, and community activism in common.

One woman in particular is still a force in my life, she my daughter's Godmother, and we have partnered in a couple business ventures. She, too, is an Alpha Woman who is a great example, besides my mother, on how to live an "Alpha Life." She taught me how to push through the noise, to work even when my bank account was not aligned with the vision, and to be honest with what I want in life.

She has never attempted to discourage me; instead, she has always tried to help me work through my witty inventions. She is a true friend because even when it seemed I went astray from the person she came to admire, her patience during my processes of growth is the reason I am the woman I am today. I know when my mother is no longer physically present in the body, this Alpha Woman will always be by my side pushing me toward purpose.

Friendship with an Alpha Woman can be a joy when you can appreciate what she brings to the table. An Alpha Woman is compassionate, honest, and super-driven yet she desires everyone connected to her to win. An Alpha Woman enjoys helping a person live a fulfilled life by making your conceptuall idea and imagination a reality. An Alpha Woman is very concrete in her method of making sure everyone around her is living a meaningful life daily. An Alpha Woman enjoys bragging about the achievements of her friends so truly being a friend with an Alpha Woman means you are up for the challenge of fulfilling your purpose in life.

An Alpha Woman is loyal, maintains integrity, and gives sound insight to those who cherishes her wisdom. An Alpha Woman does not restrict your exploration either. She understands that life is a rollercoaster. She appreciates being employed to support the ones she loves through trials, tribulations, and trauma.

I recall having a few people in my life who I called friend and one thing that I appreciate is knowing that every person that I came in contact with is in my life for a reason during a season. An Alpha Woman knows a season is not measured by calendar days or a time on a clock. A season for an Alpha Woman is business as usual. She realizes that when people come into her life, especially when she is striving to accomplish her goals, people serve a purpose.

Once this purpose is fulfilled, an Alpha Woman is not surprise when these people physically are no longer present. She has no love lost, no hate for them, nor animosity because she realizes that people need people when it makes sense. An Alpha Woman does not hold people hostage once people have fulfilled their season in her life.

Tips for Maintaining a Friendship with an Alpha Woman

- Be honest with her at all times... don't just agree with everything she says or does.
- Be genuine in your interactions with her.
- Don't allow people to tear her down privately then smile in her face publicly... she doesn't like being a fool or sucker.
- Support her dreams, help connect her dots, and buy from her.
- Don't be a person who can be bought to sabotage her.
- Embrace your own purpose in life and articulate your vision... she wants you to win too.
- Communicate with her but don't attempt to confront her in public.

- Be true to your friendship with her. When you think it is time to take a break do so without undue stress.
- Don't allow your other family, friends and associates to disrespect her.
- When she is in a vulnerable state, protect her even from herself.

Romance

It is said that a man is only as good as the woman he has by his side. Eve was the epitome of strength, uplift, and standing in her truth. Everyone wants to find their soulmate, to live life with their best friend, and to level up with a committed partner; however, it seems to take a lifetime for an Alpha Woman to experience her soulmate. It is funny how when a man needs to get things done, he secures the help of an Alpha Woman. Yet, when he wants to feel like a "man," he parades around a weaker woman who will accept his mediocre self.

It is something about a man who presents himself as an Alpha Man to compliment an Alpha Woman's flare. I am talking about a man who seems to have standards, who is sure of himself, and who cheers for you as you slay the world. This representative does not last in the company of an Alpha

Woman too long because she has a way of illuminating a man's true self of insecurity, weakness, and hate for God's punishment (to work all of his days). A man approaching a woman for lustful activities comes a dime a dozen. Yet, securing a partner to offer pure romance can be challenging victory an Alpha Woman may never meet.

There seems to be a misperception from some men that being with an Alpha Woman is difficult requiring him to conquer her into submission. Why conquer her when you can partner with to live a more abundant life. An Alpha Woman requires her mate to have a thoughtful plan, honesty, communication, and accountability. While for some men, conquering an Alpha Woman is their mission.

This mission is dangerous as, in the end, the Alpha Woman will devour a man who manipulates her womanhood. I recall a few instances in which a man attempted to dim my light to boost his manhood. I had my own moments of uncertainty regarding the difference of love versus admiration. There was one relationship specifically where I attempted to mold him into a man who would complement my Alpha energy. It was during that time that I experienced domestic violence, verbal abuse, and complacency in a relationship with a man who presented himself as an Alpha Man but was nothing more than a defected beta type. The moment I realized the relationship was fueled with his jealousy from the core of him, I knew my Alpha Woman had to stand try because she cannot do that talking down to, making her doubt herself, or even questioning her position in the relationship. I know what you are saying, "he is just insecure." I would have to agree.

Many men have "mommy issues" and decide to deflect their disappointments with their mother on to every Alpha Woman who gives them a chance romantically. A man who has to feel needed all the time is not a man for an Alpha Woman because she has limited time to wonder what tasks can she delegate to her man for him to feel complete.

Tips for partnering romantically with an Alpha Woman:

- Give her space because she embraces her freedom.
- Remain secure in yourself and agenda.
- Support her by helping to connect her dots.
- If you do have it, say it… she cannot stand wasting time and energy.

- Don't try to make her submit to you... be a leader and true to self... her respect will follow
- Know this woman will not do nor be like any woman you have experienced before.
- Hear her and genuinely listen before you attempt to "fix it."
- Don't watch her struggle... sometimes you have to lead from behind.
- Don't be a "yes dear" all the time... she wants to know you can take a stance for something.
- Sex might not happen as much as you would like; trust me she will come when it is appropriate.
- Ultimatums are not a good look as you will not be selected over her purpose.

Family

One of the most complicated relationships that an Alpha Woman has is with her family. Let's be honest there's that one woman in your family who some love while others hate her very existence. There are people in the family who talk down about her, spend tireless energy to amplify her shortcomings, and try to turn everyone against her. This woman is energetic, well accomplished, and carefree of the family's nonsense. As an Alpha Woman I have learned my focus should remain on developing and on growing beyond the generational curses which run in my family—The curses of poverty, trickery, laziness, and struggle must end with me.

There comes a point when you realize the many unfulfilled dreams and purposes within your family. Self-reflection brings a realization that no matter your age, you have the ability and the power to change the trajectory of your life. Rarely do you find a family that is full of alpha men and women who are pushing each other to stretch beyond their potential.

Many families have that one or a few Alpha men or women who are the black sheep because their light shines brighter, they move to the beat of their own drum, and/or they care more about their own peace than that of the family. These shunned Alpha Men and Women know interacting with a group of people who have a limited belief system is detrimental to their own progression and peace of mind.

When I was sixteen, I had experienced a violent rape which left a massive amount of scar tissue affecting my ability to reproduce. It was during the years I focused on my infertility where interacting with people was a challenge. My drive was to achieve by any means necessary to prove my ability to do something. Fifteen years later, I discovered God's promise of childbirth was my reality. I was overjoyed yet terrified because for years I was comfortable with being the "fun auntie." You know, the auntie without kids, who arrives to the "family gatherings" whenever she showed up, loud, openly opinionated wishing someone would check her, but in private struggled to cope with things she could not control.

Even through her pain, this auntie is the voice of reason and strength for her family. You have an auntie or two who you admire no matter what negative views people try to share with you about her. You love her because from what you can see, she has beat the odds and broken the generational curses of the family. Now that I have been blessed with the position as a mother, I realize you will learn a lot from allowing your family to support you during the journey of parenthood.

One of the greatest shifts in my life is the ability to communicate and articulate my vision to create a healthy social, emotional, and physical environment for my child with my family. It is exciting to see them overjoyed by the next stages of growth and development of my child. It seems there is a newfound admiration from the family in which they no longer attempt to "mold" me outside of my God-given character.

An Alpha Woman knows when to solicit sound advice and a helpful hand. She is okay being in a vulnerable state, especially when tracking in unknown territory. Motherhood taught me to release the "super human" mindset so my child could experience life abundantly. Have you ever seen someone who tries to do everything themselves when they know help is needed?

There is a difference between someone not having a choice to handle it all versus those who can leverage a support system to provide relief.

Here are a few things an Alpha Woman embraces while living unapologetically beyond generational curses:

- She realizes her shortcomings rather early in life.
- She finds ways to work with what she has instead of worrying about is missing
- She finds a way to strengthen the weaknesses that she inherited from her family.
- She has compassion for her family so she knows judging them will not help.

- She is always there to lend a hand to help you be better.
- She is there to rescue her loved ones even if it means providing resources or protecting them.
- She refuses to grant access to her intimate space and her journey of growth to people who see her as a "cash cow."

Recently, I have been screening calls from a particular family member who I would care not to be connected to, not even by family relations but unfortunately, we are kin. It seems like every week this person is reaching out to me via social media trying to be seen some way somehow. This is the same individual who when my grandfather was ill, was abusing drugs, stealing money from our grandparent, and indulging in some reckless behaviors which poorly reflects the family ties.

As a young girl I observed his behaviors and I knew that he truly didn't mean me any good then and surely does not mean me good now because if he was to rob the sick what would he do to a healthy, ambitious, thriving individual who has the world as her oyster?

To protect my space, future opportunities, and legacy I will not grant this person access into my world (outside of what is discovered on public media outlets). It may sound harsh but trust me family are people too. When I spoke about it to other family members there were some mixed reviews. A few who I admired deeply applauded me for standing my ground; while others believe I need to give the family member a chance because he might have changed.

You would think I have Oprah money at my disposal the way this person tries to connect with me. This behavior could be credited to the fact people want to connect to an Alpha Woman as soon as she is rising to the occasion. Everyone wants to eat even when the perceived stages of building are "complete." Most people are not here for the marathon of success, but moreover are equipped to onlook until it is time to reap some benefits.

It is no one else's responsibility to ensure an Alpha Woman's space is protected but hers because the legacy of greatness depends on her standing for something and not falling for anything. An Alpha Woman is God's gift to the world. She should be handled with care because she has an assignment from God to complete. When she is distracted from her mission, watch chaos break out.

Tips for Cultivating Family Relations with an Alpha Woman

- Support her vision.
- Be honest about the generational curses which exist in your family.
- Know she will create family ties outside her bloodline.
- Do not attempt to force her to acknowledge you as family, especially in public settings.
- Just because you are blood family doesn't mean she will be completely vulnerable with you.
- Respect her grind.
- Call her outside of funerals, you needing money, or you wanting her to do something for you. Be genuine and have a relationship.
- If you don't have anything nice to say, then don't say anything at all.
- Have her back, especially when the rest of the family is coming against her.
- Know she hears from an entity beyond this world so trust her insight; no she is not looney.
- Celebrate her successes without being asked and comfort her when sorrow arises in her life.
- Support when things are going well and when things take a turn for the worst.

- Do not force her to interact with people she has decided are distractions.

Make Your Own Way

By LaToya Rose

An alpha woman achieves. She is a team player, a leader, and a producer of winners. She is a woman who does not take well to having her authority questioned nor with being belittled. In the professional realm. I have seen some very strong women have to change their career path, after spending years trying to climb the corporate ladder, because people ("The Good Ole Boy System") wasted her time, gave her false hope, or tried to make her do things which go against her morals.

When I was working as an employee in corporate America, I found myself trying to prove myself worthy all the time. Although my superiors thought highly of me, it was my colleagues who would go behind my back in an attempt to discredit my works, to illuminate my flaws, and to get me fired without merit.

It was in Corporate America I learned the importance of understanding the written rules of the workplace. You will always be secure as long as you are able use an official handbook, human resource manual, or other written documents to support your actions and behaviors. The consequence of leveraging these documents as ammunition to protect yourself in the workplace, retaliation and bullying is real.

I had a colleague who was a hard worker and dedicated to her position yet her boss eventually began to "keep notes" to write her up for any little mistake she might have made. After acknowledging her concerns, I gave her tips to cover her assets- her paycheck and integrity. Within two weeks, her boss called her into a room with the President and Human Resource Director of the organization.

She was quiet the whole time to hear the accusations then a paper was given to her to sign. This paper was pre-drafted stating she would resign. Now, we all know if she would have signed this her lifestyle would immediately shift. Luckily, she took with her a folder of notes and even recordings which presented the wrongdoings and bullying of her boss. The President was shocked by the behaviors she had to endure. In return, the President promoted the young lady to a different department with better pay and morale. The boss was no longer a boss at that organization after this meeting.

Favor is fair, especially when your heart is pure. Grace and mercy will follow you all your days so exercise your faith daily. As a powerful Alpha Woman, it may seem you always have to be on guard, to prove yourself, and to protect yourself in the corporate setting. There are women of certain ethnic groups, specifically the Black Woman, who is always classified and labeled as an angry, difficult woman.

Statistics have shown women are leading in operating their own businesses. After observing the effects of gender and age discrimination of a former female colleague, I decided to leave corporate America. This woman had worked for this not-for-profit for over twenty-six years without having any other jobs during that time. On a Monday, she placed her frozen dinners for the week in the staff freezer but on Thursday morning, without notice, was giving paperwork her position was dissolved.

She was less than seven days from turning sixty-five and six-months from retiring from the company. How devastating is it to give all your energy to a job only to receive a small "severance pay" and to loss your pension plan? After a couple of years of rediscovering herself, she found her way in entrepreneurship.

Her freedom of time and the stability of knowing her employment security solely depends her ability to secure contracts. When I asked her how life was treating her, she replied "Being let go was the best motivation I needed to never place my destiny in one person's hands again."

Four months before I turned thirty years old, I was fed up with corporate America. I was fed up with the good ole boy system. I was fed up with knowing what my passion was but being subjected to a schedule of mundane activities daily. I made up in my mind that I would become a full- time entrepreneur before I turned thirty years old.

The best decision that I ever made in my entire life was to start working diligently for seven months, to post a written resignation letter on my mirror, and closing all of my client cases at my job before walking away. Two weeks before I took the leap of faith, I cleaned out my desk and started booking my calendar for the following quarter. It was such a liberating experience sending an email of resignation because I felt as though I had taken back my power from every unnecessary staff meeting, every bcc e-mail sent to sabotage me, and to every racist client who attempted to make me feel uncomfortable.

I knew financially I was not prepared to just take my time with entrepreneurship; therefore, creating cash flow was critical. There have been some challenges having to eat what you hunt, but it is more rewarding. The freedom of time, creativity, and collaboration is what keeps me doing what I do. Now more than ever am I celebrated for my strengths and Alpha Woman powers in the entrepreneur world.

Yet, statistics are alarming when it indicates the earnings of entrepreneur women, especially black women, are lower than our counterparts. Maybe there is a barrier with articulating value, clarity of the fair market price for services offered, or even confidence to ask for the big number.

Personally, the minute I created a clear process for interacting with a specific group of clients and offering them a meaningful product then and only then did the consistent sales begin. The problem with maintaining such a process and system for making money dealt with this profit ceiling. Yes, it is a generational curse to cave into poverty and limited beliefs related to money.

Remember the Election night of the 2016 Presidential Election? Hillary Clinton had a glass ceiling made with balloons that would separate when the ceiling opened upon her win. Unfortunately, she did not win that night nor did the ceiling open yet it seems that missed victory did not stop women as a whole. We are moving mountains with legislation, economics, business, and community engagement.

Ways to Break the Profit Ceiling

- Get Clear about who you serve and why you serve them.
- Articulate your value and leverage testimonies/references.
- Ask for referrals and new business.
- Always speak about your business.
- If you are not marketing your brand, why should others support?
- Invest in branding, marketing, and advertising to grow your business.

- Do not deviate from the process and making exceptions to your process with cost you greatly in the future.
- Sit to your standard and don't accept all money... it cost more in the future.
- Collaborate with others who can help you achieve your goals.
- Do not be afraid to price yourself at the industry standard rates.
- Hire qualified people to help you secure your sells and to collect unpaid invoices.
- Do not play about your revenue because bills have to be paid monthly.
- Hire a business coach, financial coach, advisor, and mentor so you can stay on track.

There came a time in my business where I was just hustling any and every service people said they needed. This year I had to "forgive" over twenty-five thousand dollars in unpaid invoice balances. My consistency with following the systems and processes in place for my business was non-existent for a while because my bills were coming faster than people were paying.

The issue was I started letting my personal emotions around rejection dictate how was operating in the business. Personally, I was not paying my invoices to coaches which in turned attracted "clients" who were giving me the same medicine I was serving my coaches. As an Alpha Woman, it may be hard to believe you get what you put out but that is a fact. When you take for grant the good- time, effort, and money from others, you will find yourself running on a hamster wheel.

Professionally, it can be challenging being Alpha Woman. Yes, there are some challenges. No, you do not need to apologize for being an Alpha Woman. No, you do not have to apologize for knowing and leveraging the rules especially when it will keep you out of hot water. No, it is not ok for someone to crush your spirits nor to distract you from your goals.

Understand that being an alpha woman means finding harmony within yourself and maintaining peace within your space. Know you are valuable, you are rare, and your Alpha strength is needed to make this world remain on its axis.

Tips to Be Profitable & Professional as an Alpha Woman

- Find ways to make money leveraging automations.

- Stick to a schedule for work, play, and life.
- Create a budget and stick to it.
- Plan for self-care daily.
- Find inspiration to reinvent yourself but be true to you.
- Do not get comfortable being isolated from others.
- Be open to insight from onlookers.
- Do not expect your closes friends and family members to buy from you.
- Know your numbers daily.
- Ask for the sale with confidence.
- Don't short change yourself.
- Give yourself permission to be more than you do.
- There is a difference between knowing your limits and refusing to be stretched beyond your willingness.
- Embrace professional and personal development equally.
- Take at least two days off from "working."
- Find a mentor who believes in you and is willing to develop your capabilities.
- Be vulnerable with your circle.

The Essence of an Alpha Female and Her Unbreakable Bonds

On Friendships

By Shontavia Hornsby

When making friends with other women there are an array of personalities you can encounter. There are many characters with distinct traits that tend to gravitate towards you. If we were to narrow it down into simple "animalistic" terms we have the *Alpha*, the *Beta* and the *Omega* female.

Ever since I was a child I have always attracted the alpha female as my best friends. The alpha female is often more intimidating to others, she is strong headed, bold, and nothing less than fierce. She is confrontational and stands up for what she believes. She will not take no for an answer, and things normally go her way.

An alpha female knows what she wants and likes to be in control. Alpha females put value into everything in their lives, they hold great jobs, have fabulous friends, and get the most out of life.

The Beta female is the Alpha female's right-hand woman. She will be one of the Alpha female closest friends and most trusted confidants. She is often more passive aggressive. Her personality tends to be more nurturing and sweeter. She can be confrontational and can dominate but only in dire situations.

A Beta female is never an *Alpha wannabe*, she is very comfortable with who she is. The Omega female is the last of the pack and is very smart, strong, and independent. She will have little to no ambition, not confrontational, and can lack confidence.

Intrigued by the different personality traits described for Alpha, Beta, and Omega females. I became interested in a survey for my traits. I'm not surprised with my results.

100%	Do you have Alpha Female Traits Survey
8%	**She Brings People Together** An Alpha woman may be the central "hub" in her social circle and loves to connect people. In a group scenario she will conduct the crowd around her like an orchestra. In any situation, she can find common ground, can calm tensions, and inspire great conversation. *You'll be able to spot a true Alpha in any social setting, as everyone around her will keep looking in her direction for social cues.*
10%	**She Stands Up for What She Believes In** A lot of people try to silence powerful women by insulting or threatening them, and this lady will have none of that. She's not the type to be arrogant, but, has a strong sense of justice and responsibility, and will not hold her tongue in the face of injustice. This may cause others to consider her "difficult," but really, it's just that she isn't a coward, mindless, obedient sheep who's happy to follow the rest of the flock. She knows her own mind, she has educated herself on the subjects that are important to her, and she will be proactive with issues that keep her inner fire burning. *You'll often find Alpha women in community outreach programs, or various non-profit organizations that serve the greater good.*
19%	**She Is Resilient** Life might have kicked her down a few times, but she has clawed her way back out of whatever situation she's found herself in. She may have dealt with illness, injustice, abusive situations, poverty, or any other number of devastating setbacks, but she has persevered through it, and will again, if need be. Through it all, she will maintain a sense of purpose – even optimism – and *she will not give up.*
12%	**She Is Loyal to Her Tribe** If you have earned the love and loyalty of an Alpha female, you can rest assured that she considers that to be sacred. She will be protective of you, stand by your side when you need her, and will be there for you through thick and thin. If she makes a promise to you, she will keep it no matter what. She may have many acquaintances, but the typical Alpha female only has a few very close friends whom she has allowed into the inner sanctum. Although she can establish a rapport with just about anyone, as she treats all around her with respect and courtesy, she doesn't trust easily. When someone has earned her trust, she'll consider them to be "family" and will do just about anything for them. *Much like an alpha wolf female, she feels a strong sense of responsibility toward those in her pack. She'll do what's needed to keep them strong, healthy, and safe.*
15%	**She Has Self-Respect and Dignity** If a true Alpha female finds herself in a situation where she would have to set aside her principles to make other people happy, you can be sure she'll put those expectations aside to maintain her self-respect. She won't compromise her principles. Similarly, she will conduct herself with a certain degree of dignity and grace. If she's of a certain age, she's unlikely to dress in her daughter's clothes to cling to youth but will instead wear clothing that makes her feel beautiful and powerful.
16%	**She Lives Her Own Truth** This woman may live an unconventional life that others may not understand and is totally okay with that. Other people may whisper about her behind her back, condemn her for not making the same life choices that they did, mock her fashion choices, and generally just not understand how she can live the way she does... but their opinions are irrelevant. *Her truth is her own. And she lives it unapologetically*
7%	**She Does Not Put Other Women Down** Some women who have been labeled as "Alphas" have a reputation for being cruel to other women around them. They're portrayed as being catty, judgmental creatures who'll degrade their subordinates at the office just to prove that they are the boss. A true Alpha has no use for such shallow nonsense. She knows who she is and how she got there, and she's far more likely to encourage those in whom she sees potential. She'll move up the ladder soon enough, and when she does, she'd like competent, confident women to follow in her footsteps. *The only time she'll look down on someone is when she's offering them a hand to help them up and has absolutely no need to bolster her own self-confidence by trying to crush someone else's.*
8%	**She Refuses to Play Games** This goes along with the fact that she'll speak her mind and express what she needs: she has absolutely no use for games and will refuse to play them. She has no patience for one-upmanship amongst her friends, power games at the office, or gossip, especially if it's malicious. If someone's trying to play hard to get in a relationship to get her to chase them, she'll likely say "f*ck that," get some take-out, and spend a night pampering herself. She won't engage in passive aggression, or attempts to make someone else jealous if she feels she's not getting enough attention. She has no qualms about being very open and communicative about how she feels and what she needs, and expects others to behave with a similar level of maturity. In a partnership – whether business or personal – she needs an equal. Not someone who'll try to dampen her flames, nor someone who wants her to be a mother figure. She may have already run those gauntlets, learned from them, and said "never again."
5%	**She Will Walk Away If Need Be** An alpha female who is true to herself and her own soul's needs realizes that she is a maelstrom unto herself, and that she can walk away from anything if she needs to. A situation, a romance, if she's being mistreated or disrespected, she has no qualms about packing it in and walking away in order to be true to herself. She may be a very strong, self-confident, and powerful person, but that doesn't mean that she's unfeeling or cruel. Being an Alpha is a nature-nurture balance: some women are born with these traits, while others develop them over the course of their lives. However, a woman evolved into a true Alpha female, be sure of this: she may be quite patient and tolerant for a while, but if you push her too far, not only will she walk away, she will ensure that there is no way in hell that you will follow her wherever she's going. *If a woman is brash, domineering, demanding, or cruel to others, chances are she's not a real Alpha at all. She's likely an incredibly insecure person who's hurting on many levels, and her deep-seated issues manifest in aggressive and disrespectful behavior, rather than authentic self-assurance.*

Figure 1

~ 124 ~

My characteristic traits confirm I am defiantly an alpha female. The question is why would someone want to have a friendship with me? (Jokingly)

As I mentioned before, I have always had close alpha female friends in my life. They are the closest people to me, and I've managed to form strong and deep connections with them. Although several of them have a mixture of Beta and Omega traits, the differences still mold well within our solid bond. I have special bonds with women who have Beta and Omega traits, they bring something different to our relationship that is equally valued.

Sonya Rhodes, PhD, states in an article she wrote called *"Alpha women, Beta woman,"* that we can be a mixture of both: "Alpha? Beta? It isn't always either/or, and Alpha is not better than Beta. Far more important is the degree of each that you have in your personality. If it wasn't for the Alpha women I have met and befriended throughout my life, I would not be the person I am today.

Friendships are extremely important relationships to have. Friendships have a huge impact on our health and happiness. Good friends relieve stress, provide comfort and joy, prevent loneliness and isolation, and even strengthen our physical health. But close friendships don't just happen. Many of us struggle to meet people and develop quality connections. It's never too late to make new friends, reconnect with old ones, and greatly improve your social life, emotional health, and overall well-being. Make sure to have a solid group of friends that pour into you and not drain your soul.

Every alpha female understands her friends are her strength. Unlike men, women pay much more attention to maintaining friendships. We love to be there for our friends, and we will feel honored if they have the same sense of freedom to call us in the middle of the night telling us what bothers them.

A smart woman knows she can never succeed without important people in her life. As an alpha female, I recognize many of my friends in the following list. ☺

- **The loyal best friend**

I don't have to emphasize how important it is to have a bestie who went with you through your best and worst moments in life. You know this person is your 911 emergency contact no matter the situation. They have proved that they will never let me down.

- **The wise one**

This person is someone who always gives the best advice. Whenever I'm confused and don't know what to do, this is the first person that comes to mind because she basically holds a Ph.D. in solving problems.

- **The funny one**

This one is so important. The funny friend is the one who is always energetic, positive and ready to make everyone laugh. She is special because she can improve my mood instantly, no matter how awful my day was.

- **The one who always roots for you**

Even alpha women have bad days when we feel like nothing is going right. I'm blessed to have that one friend who always roots for me, and who never misses a chance to text before my events or special occasions. It's so valuable to always have someone who believes in you. This friend is always there to remind me of the awesome person I am, and I deserve everything I desire! Pay close attention to the people who don't cheer for you!

- **The brutally honest one**

When you're an alpha woman, a lot of people abstain from telling you the truth because they're probably afraid of your reaction. But there is this one friend who doesn't give a damn and always tells you nothing but the truth.

I reflect on a friendship I had for over 15 years. We had a special bond that I thought was unbreakable. I realized somewhere between college and new careers our lives changed and steered us down different paths.

The fact that I was becoming more of an alpha female eventually became too much for her. She couldn't handle my personal growth and made the choice to walk away from our friendship, silently, with no explanation or continued contact. This loss affected me for years and made me lury when developing new friendships. I'm certain I was a great friend, and I own up to any fault I might have caused to end our friendship.

Unfortunately, everything was never revealed. My only regret is not having the opportunity to discuss the issues and mend our relationship. Clearly what I believed to be valuable was no longer important to her. The lesson learned from this is, everyone will not understand the person you evolve into. They are only able to see and understand at their capacity, not yours.

My desire and progression in life is for me, if that is too much for others, then they were not meant to be on my journey. That relationship is missed; however, life goes on, I can only learn and grow from it.

These are the friendships that fill our souls, and bolster and shape our identities and life paths. They keep us mentally and physically healthy: good friends improve immunity, spark creativity, and even decrease our stress levels.

However, even our easiest and richest friendships can be laced with tensions and conflicts, as are most human relationships. They can lose a bit of their magic and fail to regain it, or even fade out altogether for tragic reasons, or no reason at all.

Dedication

This chapter is dedicated to my real friends, the Alpha, Beta, and Omega female's in my life. My ride or dies, the ones who've been by my side through thick and thin, through divorce and death, for birthdays and graduations, for the many business endeavors I've pursued. The friends who've been there for the laughs but, most importantly, for the tears. The friends who correct me when

I've wronged, and support me when I need it, but say I don't. The friends who inspire me, empower me, and always encourage me to level up- you never hesitate to remind me of my greatness and of the Boss I am. The friends who travel the world with me, and most of all the friends who pray with and for me!

I wouldn't be half the woman I am today without the genuine love and support each of you give me. I'm forever grateful to God for placing the right women in my life. God created a dynamic alpha female when he created me, and he knew I would need each of you on this journey.

I often ask myself, how is it that I'm blessed with so many phenomenal women in my life? How is it that every single being in my spectrum is genuine? My conclusion is, Alpha women attract what we are. We are all unique, but we have learned to give what we each need. While building our relationships, we respect each other's flaws, never judging and always uplifting.

Competition and jealously is never an issue as everyone have "Boss lady confidence" and walks boldly in their purpose. We don't need validation of others; self-value is more than enough. Our relationships have been tested yet nurtured and blossomed into amazing treasures. My prayer is that I am to each of you, what you are to me. ***Humbly Blessed!***

An Alpha Female Will Always Prevail!

On Careers

By Shontavia Hornsby

f you adhere to the ideologies associated with *Alpha*, *Beta*, etc. traits in both male and female personalities, chances are you've been led to believe that an alpha female shows certain aggressive and domineering behaviors. Alpha women have been described as bossy, manipulative, condescending, and emasculating, but those are usually traits exhibited by people who desperately want to be in control but aren't.

A real Alpha female may have a strong personality, but what makes her a leader, what inspires her diligence and tenacity, is a strong sense of self, and of purpose!

As a young woman, I recognized I possessed many characteristics of an alpha female. I'm strong, talented, highly motivated, and unapologetically embrace self-confidence and leadership ambitions. Most importantly, my purpose and life passions are impactful!

Being an alpha female, in my 20-year corporate career, has proven to be challenging at times in the work place. I am truly grateful for one experience that changed the trajectory of my career. New leadership can make or break an organization. My new boss at a Fortune 500 company took quick action setting the tone for our organization. Her unprofessional acts to belittle, chastise, and unjustly accuse me of committing horrific mistakes.

The actions where obvious as she frequently did this in public as an act for embarrassment. In meetings, she would dismiss my ideas without discussion and even cut me off in mid-sentence. I started to hear about meetings to which I wasn't invited but felt I should be.

She repeatedly denied my approval to attend conferences and training seminars. Being in a leadership position myself, I noticed I was excluded from my boss' small circle of confidants and other leadership events. My boss was determined to sabotage me and my career. Her actions made it difficult for me going to work where I once loved, to an unhealthy and stressful atmosphere.

At this moment I realized I was a THREAT to her! My boss struggled with the fact that I was a young, black, educated woman, powerful alpha female. She was determined to bring it all to an end.

Unfortunately, she underestimated my power as an alpha female!

After dealing with her many unprofessional antics for months. I decided it was time to stand up for myself. My reaction was full of anger, confusion, and frustration. However, I realized I must handle everything professionally and with class. I feared my reputation would suffer, and that my job was in jeopardy.

In my 20 years of service with this company, I have never worked with any boss who displayed this type of work ethic. I took pride in my commitment, dedication, and performance in every position I held within the organization. In addition, I built strong professional relationships with my prior leadership, many taking the initiative to mentor and groom me for career advancement. My goal was to grow professionally and provide the best service to our customers. Having the support from prior leadership allowed room for success. The new leadership had different objectives for my role.

I did nothing to provoke my boss and the verbal attacks and treatment seemed so unfair. What likely triggered my boss's bad behavior is the fact that I was great at what I did; I was considered a top performer. I was an expert in my position, had goals to continue advancing up the leadership ladder, in addition to having a wealth of company knowledge and cultural experience.

The realization of my boss seeing me as a threat opened my eyes to the world of women who hate other women- alpha females. This was my first experience dealing with something like this on a professional level and I was extremely shocked!

There are potentially two major factors contributing to my boss's toxic behavior. The first is *psychological*. Her behavior might have been driven by her insecurity. She didn't believe that her own innate abilities would help her reach her career goals. Another factor is *the workplace itself*. A male dominated workplace sets women up to compete due to increased scrutiny and a scarcity of top leadership positions for women. The psychological factors along with the workplace culture together create female rivalry at its ultimate level.

Research confirms that when women lack confidence in innate talent to help us reach our goals, we are more competitive, and anyone is a potential threat, especially other women in a workplace that fails to offer enough advancement opportunity.

Katherine Crowley and Kathi Elster, co-authors of Mean Girls at Work: How to Stay Professional When Things Get Personal, state that, "Women are complicated. While most of us want to be kind and nurturing, we struggle with our darker side - feelings of jealousy, envy, and competition. Women often compete more covertly and behind the scenes. This competition and indirect aggression is at the heart of mean behavior among women at work."

My expectation is for women to collaborate and mentor each other to be successful. But that's not necessarily what happens. The dark toxic side is triggered by the increased scrutiny that women experience. The female rivalry is fueled by a workplace culture that does not provide a level playing field for women, equal pay, and/or equal opportunity for women to reach leadership positions.

This situation was taking a toll on me, I had to detach emotionally. I realized I was allowing this woman and her behavior towards me to take away my power. Constantly stressing over the unfairness of this situation also stemmed from feeling out of control. It was consuming too much of my energy. My attitude of going into the office changed for the worse, I contemplated changing my career, and leaving to work for another company.

I struggled with focusing on what I could control in a positive, productive, and professional manner. I was miserable, unproductive and in a fearful place every day because I realized her goal was to manage me out. My boss didn't have valid proof to back up her accusations regarding my work performance. Neither did she have valid reason to terminate me, so she did everything in her power to make my daily work experience as horrible as possible.

If you know one thing about an alpha female, you know she refuses to play games. An alpha female is a BOSS, an alpha female will speak her mind and express what she needs, she will take charge and go after what she wants, especially if she feels like someone is coming to destroy her. An alpha female will not take no for an answer and will bulldoze through anyone who stands in her way. My boss has now activated "beast mode" in this alpha female!

My immediate reaction was to build a power network to protect my reputation. I took steps to reconnect with the team, other leaders, and key stakeholders. Since having prior relationships with many, I made sure they understood my value in case my boss offered negative comments about me.

In addition, I met with Human Resource for protection and to get advice on how to navigate around my boss's toxic behavior as well as advice on how to deal with it professionally. I knew presenting my case to HR could be challenging, as they expect management to conduct business in a professional manner and will usually support higher leadership over any other employees.

My expectations of leadership and HR was something of high standards and fairness, clearly this was not the case of either performing with honest professionalism. No actions were taken to help resolve the issues at hand. Since I am an alpha female, I have extreme confidence and ability of taking care of business for myself. I immediately "leveled up" and took actions in my own hands. Alpha females do not sit back and wait for others to handle the situation, they boldly step up and take care of the problem, with or without the help of others.

My career was in jeopardy, everything I worked hard for and contributed to the company was at risk. One rule to always follow as an alpha female is, never wait for someone else to take care of your needs. You are responsible for your own direction and path in life, take charge and never apologize for doing what is best for you.

As I began implementing my plan of action, I identified my value proposition so that I could articulate how I contribute to positive business results to leadership and those who had power and influence. I kept a success journal to document my accomplishments and project performances. I continued to act and perform as an alpha female would.

I strived to be a role model for collaboration over competition. As a leader myself, I praised other women on their work performance, continued to mentor women as I felt it was important to show there are women leaders in the workplace that do support them in their career progression. The derailment plans my boss had for me positioned me to take my leadership abilities to the next level.

We expect women to help support our advancement, but the reality is that insecurities along with the competitive nature of the workplace set the stage for female rivalry. We can't control other people's bad behavior. We can only control our own reaction to that behavior. We must realize that toxic people rob our power and we can't let them!

Focus on the things we can control to protect our reputation and remain positive and productive is how an alpha female will boldly take back control.

The outcome of this situation is unfortunate for the company. I made the bold decision to leave a place that nurtured me professionally for 20 years. Taking charge of my future positioned me join a new company with higher salary and leadership position. The unprofessionalism of my boss caused the Fortune 500 company to lose highly skilled professionals as other co-workers left as well.

When she thought she won, she only destroyed the reputation of the organization as new, non-qualified employees joined to fill the positions of employees who had expertise and 15-20-year tenure within the company.

We are living in a time when women are beginning to shine and succeed at the highest levels, on their own terms. As an alpha female I am a very ambitious woman. I face extra challenges and tend to see my experience and qualifications played down or ignored because people can't handle what I bring to the table.

I'm told that, as a woman with ambition, I should double down, I'm doing too much, I am extreme at times. Yes, I am bossy, yes, I am very independent, yes, I am a leader and not a follower, yes, I have extremely high self-confidence, yes, I care less of other's opinion about me.

Yes, people are usually intimidated by me and immediately form their own negative opinions without getting a chance to know me. However, I understand my boldness as an alpha female requires a level of elevation and separation. I ignore the misconceptions and stay focused on my purpose.

My characteristics and actions as an alpha female always prove to empower and uplift the next woman, never belittling or degrading a woman. I firmly believe there is enough room at the top for everyone willing to work hard and get there. I will never apologize for being a BOSS, I am bold and courage's, I am an alpha female!

Thank you "ex- boss", for releasing this alpha woman to her destiny!

Kissing Frogs

By Stephanie A.

To be an alpha woman is to be attributed some amazing extraordinary qualities, that often cause those around you to wonder and celebrate in awe or mumble under their breath with thoughts that stem from envy or their own deep-rooted insecurities.

For each of us it is different, things that are important to me may not be important to another alpha woman and I get that. We are all made differently with purpose. I personally have spent years working to ensure that my heart is the single most extraordinary quality that I possess. It is the way I want to be remembered and defined. I believe that everything else will radiate from that one place.

Sure, I may also have certain physical beauties, smarts, character, and present with a very polished demeanor. It may even appear to others as if I have it all together. While I do have a sincere gratitude for the way that I can wake up and approach each day, each challenge and all the mountains that I have moved or will move in this lifetime. I'm human and I feel. Just like everyone else, I long to be cherished in an amazing intimate relationship.

Very seldom do I or other strong women feel comfortable discussing the places in us that we may deem weak. I know that for myself and probably true for many other women, given the current climate of today's dating culture, emotions and negative perspective surrounding this topic can be particularly high.

It is almost as if it is just so much easier to stay focused on building and making great things happen in life then to expose oneself to this level of vulnerability. I often found that to be very difficult. Yes, I do think that it is important that I protect my peace and the plans I have for my future. I also think that it is equally important that I have someone to share and do life with.

For many years I'd given up on the possibility of true commitment and finding a great man of my own. I am sure that we can all admit that, that is a feeling that can come and go depending upon the direction of the wind.

This does not mean that I have been that angry, overly independent woman who doesn't need a man as many alpha women have been described. It simply means that I dated without the expectation of outcome. I enjoyed my time and the value exchanged in those shared life experiences and when things were over, I wasn't lost in that place of personal defeat due to a failed relationship.

I rationalized that thought for years by inserting the idea that I had too much going on in my life that required greater levels of my attention. While I know that there was some truth in that I also recognize the wall that I put up in my mind as a protection mechanism. I used that idea to deal with any level of rejection as it related to men not meeting my expectations or the weight of my life's plate at that time being heavier than they were comfortable with taking on.

Sometimes we just have to get real with ourselves about where we are, what we need and what we actually have to offer another person. Yes, I am pretty sure that I was born with an alpha personality, but life and its experiences further shaped the path I would as an alpha woman walk.

I would find myself meeting men who were just as unavailable as I was. I was busy being an amazing single mother, building a corporate career and being a caretaker for my disabled Mom, at the end of the day I would always find great men even well-established men, but who were equally as busy.

The intention was there, but time was not. I felt like if I devoted too much attention to the person of interest then my obligations fell short. If he was more invested than me, it was always an issue of me showing lack of interest and a clear point of my inability to be able to commit to a relationship.

Sure, over time we would have probably been able to create ways to make each other's loads easier but because of time, I could never arrive at that level of comfort. I had to develop a certain level of acceptance about where my life was, and that it was easier to enjoy having someone who wanted to be there as much as I wanted to be, without the constant pressure of moving forward in some level of commitment. I looked at it as at least having a piece of what I wanted without being completely alone.

Over time there was always a desire for more on his side or mine and depending upon how long we had played the roles that we were in without the commitment it seemed to always end in a redundant cycle of trying to evolve to something that the relationship itself had kind of already surpassed in time.

The process was real and taught me a lot. I, just like many others started with some crazy list of what this person needed to have in order for me to be fulfilled, happy and committed. Only to have to face my own reality of truth.

Everyone desires companionship, there is something special about finding someone who wants to share and do life together. The part that makes it all unique is that every person has a different concept of what the ideal mate looks and feels like. The even greater part is that it only has to make sense to you and that person.

I found that I sometimes struggled with the concept of public perception. I was often held to a high level of expectations concerning life in general. It's not always easy when the world sees you as holding it all together and random single or married men make comments to you about how lucky your husband is etc. because of the way that you carry yourself.

Aren't you supposed to dress and carry yourself for the role that you want not the role that you have? In many instances I would just shrug and smile. It wasn't worth the explanation and he probably wasn't him anyways.

Dating as an alpha had its challenges and sometimes lonely lengths of singleness. I would bump heads with men who felt like I was too strong, too opinionated, too set in my own ways of thinking and doing. In some instances, there may have been some truth to that. I would from time to time evaluate myself with all seriousness in attempt to become both masterfully strong in my character yet soft and delicate to ensure that I was handled a certain way, as a point of personal improvement.

Over time I matured, life and circumstances changed, and I developed a new-found desire in wanting to be a great woman to someone someday. I felt like the key to that was to always remain teachable. Other times I would find myself completely frustrated with the process.

A man's initial interest and approach versus the way he did or did not express his intentions and his ability to follow thru and remain consistent. I was hardening soft places inside of me. I became very nonchalant and callus towards certain personality types. The more that I learned about what I actually needed from a partner thru personal experience, the more important I found it to study the character of men opposed to their look and what they brought to the table. This had been a common place of personal error. Yes, of course physical attraction is important, but maybe its order of importance should not have been as close to the top of the list as it was.

I realized that I was spending too much of my time kissing frogs and making them happy in hopes that they would turn into my prince, for lack of better words. There were days I found myself giving men too much of my attention and energy to a point of distraction from my life's goals. What I did conclude is that I had to be certain of what I needed from this person of interest as I possessed many of the qualities that each of these men desired in their potential mate. I had to be a quick decider on the characteristics that were important to me in my partner and if they possessed them or not.

There is nothing more disheartening then months of dating, wasted efforts and loss of finances on an investment with lack of return. I do try to always respect other peoples, time effort and money. Don't get me wrong some of these frogs had some amazing package deals, security and promise, but majority of the time they lacked the character that I needed to see myself solid in a committed relationship. I was not a princess that needed to be saved from the castle protected by the dragon. I was a queen who was used to running shit, I was ready for a king strong, willing and able to be my equal and help call some shots.

Dating got discouraging and I disconnected. I wasn't looking to be someone's temporary happiness or waste my time getting dolled up to feel like I was dying all night listening to a man talk us thru dinner. Two or three hours that I could already tell from the initial conversation wasn't going anywhere.

I was looking for one man, that was an easy connection that just felt right, who understood me and was all about my details and until that day I just needed to take a break. I was over living in the idea of trying to filter thru those who expressed their interest to find the perfect him. I did however feel that it was always important to know specifically the necessary characteristics that I was looking for in my companion.

So, when he presented, I could easily cover the basics. Seeking a man with strong intellect and character sounds simple, but the substance that it would bring to our relationship would be unreal. I clutched this list like a bible tucked safely away in my fanciest purse. He needed to embody all of these traits, no short stops allowed.

- Leadership - someone who is strong enough mentally to take the wheel that I can over time trust with my life.
- Willingness to communicate - on every level without reservation.
- Intelligence - that matches or exceeds my own (Not necessarily in the form of books smarts but someone who can keep me engaged and also be a teacher.)
- Compassion - towards human kind and our overall culture.
- Interest - sharing a genuine interest in the things that are important to me, my dreams and visions that I have for the future.
- Drive - strong desire to accomplish something greater together. Not someone who is stuck on solo wealth creating missions.
- Spiritually in tune - sharing beliefs, seeing value and seeking understanding in the why behind things that are unknown.

- Mentally available - does this person have room for a committed relationship in their life.

It is true when they say love will find you when you least expect it. As an alpha woman that can be difficult since, we typically try to control our emotions and availability to others based on our own wants and desires. I fell in love with the idea of "working on the queen that I desire to be while I wait for my king to appear."

I had to constantly remind myself when the plight of being single would get the best of me. That being an alpha woman didn't make me any less delicate or deserving of someone amazing to share my life with. Someone who loved and cherished me like the rarest pearl found in the sea. Someone who was both strong and kind, but certain of his want of me.

My alpha did however make me strong enough endure the wait for my true help mate to arrive without losing myself by settling for another temporary level of comfort in the wrong person.

The biggest mis-education of an alpha woman in this light is that we are free from the pains and struggles associated with finding companionship. That we are overbearing and not also in need of the truest form of love in a relationship. I've learned personally that being an alpha woman doesn't make us immune to life's realness, it just helps us to shape the way that we respond to disappointment. The way that we react to things not working in our favor.

Our ability to overcome obstacles and challenges, and the way that we will pick ourselves up and still be seen in the light as strong willed amazing women who will not be defeated from one issue to the next. I use my own personal walk and story to change the hearts of many people surrounding the social norms of real love when dealing with an Alpha woman.

I encourage all women, but more specifically my alpha sisters to continue to walk in your greatness. Be easy on yourself in places of weakness or that you find yourself particularly fragile. Understand that you are just as deserving and loveable as the next woman with or without your genetic badass superwoman cape. Great things happen for those who remain true and consistent.

Finding My Alpha Worth

By Stephanie A.

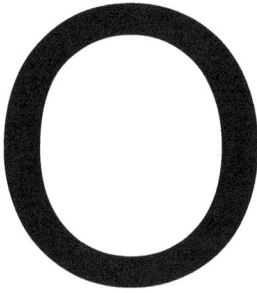

One of the first things that people recognize about me, or any other woman, is confidence or lack thereof. It is the one-character trait that people can begin judging you on as soon as they see you, even before you open your mouth to speak.

I have always viewed my level of self-confidence as a great character asset. I take much pride in the way that I believe in my personal ability to be great and do good work. Little did I know that learning to properly position myself to have my passions seen in the right light would be one of my life's greatest challenges and lessons.

It all started when I was old enough to work at the age of 15. That was a milestone of independence for me. I remember immediately telling my father that I wanted to get a job! I needed to make my own money and be able to purchase for myself all the things my parents didn't see a need for and so I worked. My first job at the frozen custard stand was the beginning of the development in who I was to become.

Sure, it was just a part- time job making ice cream sundaes, but it was the segway into my paying my own way, to obtain many of my life's firsts, amongst many other self-empowering moments. It was the first step in being outside of my family unit and learning how to interact with all kinds of people, people who I might add would do anything for the last pint of butter pecan.

I loved that job! Right along with the perks and popularity of working in the spot light of one of the city's hot spots. I was proud of myself going to school, working and still playing high school sports. I was a go getter and my efforts were admired.

In my early 20's as I began to grow and develop in my professional life in the corporate world, my view surrounding self-confidence went thru some changes. During this stage of life, I was still surrounded by groups of people who loved me and thought I was great in one way or another, but they knew that it was time for me to set out into the real world. Many of who would still encourage me to go out and live my best life.

"Sky is the limit" they say, "Shoot for the stars and maybe you will land on the moon." Or they would turn their noses and question if I had stepped outside of my league. Insinuating that maybe I should be more realistic with things that I wanted and that I might need to work my way up to this or that.

Starting smaller was safe and a better idea. I listened as they spoke their own life's fears into my story. Tuh! That only added fuel to my fire. Trying to discourage me from something that I thought I should have was almost like an "I bet you can't" dare amongst young children. Eagerly I set out to accomplish every can possible.

To me there was no greater feeling than walking into a company of my desire, seeking out positions that I believed I was empowered to be great in and securing the bag. Either instantly or by the time I made it back to my vehicle if not shortly thereafter.

Some of which worked out wonderfully and are still pillars in my foundation of work ethic and history, then there are others that came to devastating ends. I found that during this time my confidence and my age posed as problem. While my eagerness and skill set made me, a young know it all. I was learning the hard way that in Corporate America. Too much confidence would pitch me into some corners, I was not prepared to be in. While it would encourage and promote my male peers. It took me years to understand what was happening during times of employable disconnections, whether I quit or was fired.

I was learning that the very thing that got me hired on the spot, and had people so excited about me in the interview was also the same reason why I was being called into the office; being written up for someone else's opinion of me, not my work. I was learning why I was constantly being chastised or praised for the way my personality rallied those around me for both good and bad. **I was held responsible for the morale of the masses**, in the event that I appeared anything less than happy in my environment or felt there was some level of unjust taking place.

I can't even begin to tell you how old that conversation got. I found myself shrinking. I felt my confidence in who I was, what I believed, and my skill set just diminishing into the background of trying to make a living and be an adult. I needed that pay check to provide life. So, there I sat quietly, diligently producing great work, trying to maintain a very stale version of self in order to keep a low profile. I was learning that it was not ok to be my authentic self.

As I moved into my late 20's early 30's I noticed when I interviewed for different positions that something new was happening during interviews. I'd walk in, introduce myself and immediately or not long after the person or persons interviewing me would look to my left hand to see if I was married. I found it odd, and even thought I was over reacting because I felt a way about the fact that I was almost 30 and unmarried. It seemed to be a common insecurity for women of this age group after being taught for years that marriage is the goal.

For many women, and employers, marriage is a symbol of validation to the rest of the world. It is an unspoken proof that you can be a team player, that you make compromises, that you value loyalty and commitment and that someone else values you enough to partake in this level of commitment with you. I also found myself suddenly being illegally questioned about having children, not through a direct way of asking but a round about way of trying to determine if I was a mother and just how many children I might have.

The first few times this caught me off guard and I am sure that I went on raving about how amazing my child was before I realized what was happening or knew the laws concerning these types of interview questions.

Later, as I found myself working in a human resource role where my suspicions were confirmed one hiring manager's opinion at a time. I specifically remember a hiring manager tell me these 2 things, as we had only spoken over the phone and he had never seen me.

Single middle-aged black women tend to be a bit more aggressive and unwilling to compromise, it just makes them difficult to work with.

Hiring a single mother will either get us a dedicated worker for life because she needs to provide for her children or it will be a world wind of headache trying to make accommodations for a mother to take care of her kids, and business will fall behind.

I was glad at that moment that he didn't know my real story, but wow, I still stand in awe of how real and cruel judgement can be.

Forward, I find myself in a position that I had been thriving in for almost 3 years without a single issue having occurred, it was like a record for me. I was able to join the team, pick up on all training and technology within a matter of 2 weeks versus the typical 6. I was seen as a valuable team player with excellent conflict resolution that exuded all applaudable leadership qualities desired according to my last review.

'Shortly after being hired I became responsible for all new hire training, 60 employees and very little turn over. What I was certain of at this point in my career was that great leadership comes from within and it doesn't have anything to do with gender. It means taking care of people not just family or loved ones, but those who work with us and for us, too. A person who feels valued will always go above and beyond.

Then a new director was hired and within a matter of 2 months managed to have everyone up in arms, questioning if they needed to start looking for new employment. I found myself at the head of a heated conversation of which, he had me in his office yelling at me at the top of his lungs to the point that he was shaking.

We went back and forth about the appropriate way to discuss personal HR matters of employees with other employees. When I refused to back down and ended the conversation, he went to his superior and explained how he was only trying to talk to me and how I was very rude and aggressive.

Although, I explained my side of the story, clearly rattled by the experience with tears in my eyes having never had a single issue in the past, I was still written up and eventually fired within the next 6 months.

Ultimately, I was told that it was because I was displaying signs of aggressive behavior and I was no longer a good fit for the team. I was negatively impacting my work environment and being cancerous to the moral. I had to laugh aloud. Within the next 60 days, 35 employees left this department of their own free will.

This was a turning point in my life.

Not only did this experience help me to realize that there was no more room for me to play small, dumbing down my skills, character and ability in any work environment. Especially for the sake of someone else's ego or tenure. It created a sense of awareness of just how many other people face these types of issues on a day-to-day basis but are not strong enough to overcome them and are consistently subjected to the breakdown of their character and esteem in positions that they work diligently 40+ hours a week.

I promised myself that from that day forward I would never disclose to my employer that I was a single mom, for as long as I was a single mom. I didn't need that pity nor was I ever going to allow someone to think that, they had that power over me. I was making some changes to how I was playing the corporate game from here on out.

I figured that If I had allowed previous employers of my past to teach me into playing small and being less than my authentic-self, protecting my peace of mind and those that I love the most was not that different. I took time to re-calibrate and identify who I was after downplaying my intelligence and character for so long.

Building myself back up and identifying the characteristics of worthy career choices

I was on a mission, long passed were the days of me walking into interviews only listening to the employers needs of the type of person they were seeking and the pay scale being the most important part of the conversation. I was no longer afraid to let them know exactly how great I was and the ways in which I saw myself being successful in said roles.

I was also certain to ask appropriate questions that painted a clear picture of working environments and opportunities for growth. Being certain to advise the hiring manager of the ways that I work most effectively to ensure that we are a good fit for one another.

Agreed understanding that respect in a work environment is a must. I have been able to find my place within any organization that I have chosen since then. There is something special in having the ability to walk in your gifts and utilize your greatness without feeling like you are too much.

Now more than ever I was being made aware of my presence. The impact that I had on those I worked directly with and the ways I helped to shape the culture of my environment. I should not take this lightly, I remembered thinking to myself. Even though I was unemployed and unsure of my next path, I didn't have that same fear that usually sets in with the reality of that level of uncertainty.

I got up every single day for the next 2months expecting great things. Putting forward the efforts and making sure that I enjoyed every day that I was not working since we all know that those days are few and far between as an adult. The end result was a rewarding opportunity that restored me both professionally and personally. I was quickly accepted in my new environment, celebrated, valued and confident that I was in the right place at the right time.

I recognized early in my life that that I possessed the qualities of an Alpha female, but I didn't know exactly what power that held. I will say that it is a personality type that requires a lot of fine-tuning. It calls for you to be able to walk in a fearless level of leadership that makes an impact and inspires other people. It has held me to a high level of emotional awareness through both self-actualization and empathy.

I am constantly looking to seek knowledge in every opportunity be it personal experience or life challenges, professional development, or the teachings of other people. It's a desire inside of me to cultivate a certain level of harmony overall, especially after feeling as though I can easily be negatively labeled, and stereotyped because of my strong identity.

Studies say that the brain shapes itself according to repeated experiences. Growing in my Alpha professionally has given me a certain level of distinct ambition in perusing the concept of limitless possibilities. I am constantly seeking out new opportunities and the best way to make the most of this life.

It was not long after identifying in greater capacity my desire to live, work and enjoy life according to a certain moral compass. That I further understood that my gifts may not be best utilized in the environments in which I am working for someone else, but instead initiating the efforts of becoming my own boss. I was learning to move comfortably in my passions. Hell, I was even getting bold. I was ready to become a business owner.

I continued to work as I began to put the pieces of the puzzle together. My tolerance for any level of workplace foolishness was getting very short. The most complicated thing in deciding that you should step out and become your own boss are the naysayers or the uncertain faces and responses from those close to you. Those that I thought would encourage me the most.

Those that I hoped to be my greatest supporters. The responses to my hungry 30 something year old self were a lot different from the ones I received years earlier, when I graduated high school or even college. The message was different, the tone was fearful. I understood that at this point we all had been exposed to the real world and adulting was not made for the weary. People would tell me that it was a great idea and then counter act the thought with stating all the reasons why they could never be an entrepreneur.

To the weak mind, that lack of support could be a strong enough force to make you give up or send you into the black hole of lost and seeking validation. Followed by years of contemplation should have, could have, would have, if I'd only known.

For me it was just another confirmation that I was unique and called to do something different. It was time for me to get serious and step out into unfamiliar territory and see what I was able to pull out of my magic hat.

I just didn't know, what I didn't know. I hope that makes a lot of sense. I was ready to be a boss. I was eager, I had all the ambition, but I didn't know where to start. All the people who actually knew something, had zero intention on just telling me how to go out and be great. Not for free anyways!

They would pump you up and tell you it's your time and finish their statement with do your research. If you need to know how to do anything the internet is your greatest resource. (I knew that the internet was a resource, but only if you knew what you were looking for. (My favorite curse words seemed so appropriate in this moment). I would get so angry, why not just show me the way? There is enough room for us all to be great. I understood after hitting a few walls that I was going to have to invest in myself.

It is very true when they say... sometimes you get what you pay for. I promise that you will bring the greatest return of your own investment.

I buckled down and began to research and make plans of my current life simplifying in places that I could so that I would be able to dedicate more of my time towards building what in my mind was as an empire even though I was only laying the 1st bricks. I knew that the difference between this dream and the dream of the next person with similar likes had to be my undying commitment to never giving up.

I'd finally made the decision to step into a role that didn't wrap me in the vicious cycle of wanting to climb the corporate ladder. I knew that the one thing that posed as a constant barrier of what I wanted to obtain, was being in an environment where other people saw greatness in me also and constantly tried to peg me into different roles. It always seemed to turn into a vicious cycle of the longest engagement of me proving my worth and doing the work for extended periods of time before advancement and in some cases without companies ever actually putting a ring on it and making it official.

Goal setting became my new replacement to Gray's Anatomy. I was monitoring everything that I thought about. Limiting access to me and the types of conversations that I would partake in, being cautious of who I allowed to pull from my energy. Trying to eliminate things that posed as a waste of my time. I sought out new ways to enhance my craft and enrolled in different course work to make me the subject matter expert.

I promised myself that I was going to work just as hard for me as I did all my previous employers. I made realistic goals that I could celebrate if no one else was celebrating with me. Even when I attempted things and failed, I sought to find the success in each circumstance. I had arrived at a level of self-awareness that made me an incredible asset to myself. Believing in my own ability to create as

a means of income and prosperity. I can say
that I finally understood my worth.

Alpha Raised

Surviving & Thriving

By Suprena Hickman

lpha woman? Who, me? Nah, I'll pass on that one. Yes, that used to be me. You see, I never would've called myself an Alpha Woman at all. You may remember there was an old 1980's movie called The Last Dragon. In the movie, one of the main characters was called "Bruce Leroy".

Well, in this movie, Bruce Leroy was a martial artist who apparently didn't realize the power he had within him. He went throughout most of the movie looking for the master who could help him achieve the final level of his trainings.

Despite the fact that his previous master already told him he had reached the final level in his martial arts training, he went on a quest to find the one with "the glow". Well eventually, he realized that he already possessed what he was looking for. The powers were within him.

In my case, whenever I heard of an alpha woman, I never considered looking within myself. I actually always admired the alpha woman and could easily recognize them from afar, but I never surrounded myself with them.

I was actually a bit intimidated by them on the low- yet, I admired them and their drive. They were overachievers and handled their business like a boss. They were persistent, fearless, and no-nonsense! They were the super women of the world. They were the women who I felt were unstoppable and extremely resilient. That type of woman, I thought, could never be me.

Like Bruce Leroy in the movie, along my journey in life of working closely with women to help empower and heal them, I discovered that the type of women I was, both intimidated by and admired, was actually within me. You see, I was raised by an alpha woman and grew up amongst other alpha women. I was indeed alpha raised!

My momma was, and still is, that alpha woman I have described and she raised her daughters to be alpha women. I wasn't raised with a father in the home, so I always said my momma was my mother and father- so to speak. Because of her experiences as a woman growing up, and a woman hurt and raising children by herself after a divorce, she taught her kids the best way she knew. No, we never had a conversation about how to be an alpha woman. My momma doesn't even know what an alpha woman is if I asked her. What she did teach us was how to stand up and speak up for ourselves. She taught us how to be resilient and how to be strong independent women. She raised us to be tough.

Studies from Nichols College's Institute of Women's Leadership reported that women in the United States represented 47% of the workforce, and in 40% of families, women are the primary or sole breadwinner. Well, my momma never was a business owner- nor did she have some top level executive position on her job, but she was a custodian at a local college. She, however, operated her home and her live events as if she held an executive position on a job.

My momma was our sole provider in the home and a resourceful queen she was and still is. As a single parent, she was simply determined to win, and it showed in her consistent, daily actions.

Amongst the other things she taught me were invaluable business skills that I currently use. I grew up watching and helping her create events for her church and civic organizations. I was basically her administrative assistant. I had an advantage as being her youngest child and the last in the house. Therefore, I was able to witness and participate in many of her programs that she produced in the church.

She taught me how to build relationships and she taught me speaking up and stating what I wanted. She showed me what consistency looked like and the results you get from it. She also showed me what self-respect looks like as she deposited those words of encouragement.

Those words called for me to respect myself and others will naturally do the same. This is something I notice many girls and women today do not have and they tend to envy those who do have self-respect.

Oh, and my momma literally came home and cooked six to seven days per week. I learned at an early age how to set the tables, cook, and clean a home because this is what she did every night before we ate. She ran a tight ship at home and she believed in order. The house needed to be cleaned at all times. The beds needed to be made up every day with sheets folded back and the bottoms tucked in as if we were in the military.

I later revisited this lesson in nursing school. My mom was very strict on changing the linens weekly, but if someone else stayed in the bed during the week, then you changed those sheets after they left for good. She taught me the importance of being a lady with class and to respect, not only myself, but those around me as well. I was also taught how to stand in my truth and stop following the crowd and simply be myself.

I was trained to be a strong woman who was not dependent upon a man for my needs. Although she warned me a few times growing up of not depending on a man for my needs, she never talked me out of accepting assistance from a man. I grew up watching this Super Shero take care of her kids, grandkids, and anyone else needing to stay in the home temporarily.

She opened her doors to them and took care of everything from laundry, to cooking, to yard work- even cutting down trees when needed, and she still had a full time job working swing shift. I honestly don't recall her sleeping. I do know that she was and still is a beast. Well, the older I got, I realized I'm that strong woman I admired. I am my mother's child. Well, except, I didn't cut down any trees of course.

The lessons I got from my momma were simply invaluable and I apply them daily. I've grown to discover that these were all characteristics of an alpha woman. The super woman, or Super Shero, who can do nearly anything, is a bad woman! My momma is definitely who you would call a bossy woman and she is very persistent. She doesn't stop until she gets what she wants and needs. I don't think we have enough women today like this.

She is that type of woman that many guys really want, but may have problems getting, simply because of their approach or maturity level. Either they would become intimated by the alpha woman or they would pursue her even harder. Now, as I look back at those times, I guess she decided it would've been much better without a man- especially after going through a rough divorce and not having that man to help her in the home.

I honestly believe that whatever male she would have chosen, she may have been too much of a boss for him during that time. He would have likely tried to see where he would fit into her life. All men aren't equipped to handle an alpha woman. A few women, I've witnessed, simply settled in relationships for the sake of maintaining one. They dumbed themselves down in fear of emasculating their male mates and causing friction in their relationship. This makes a miserable relationship by the way.

When I think of my relationships journey, with regards to dating, I believe I definitely dumbed myself down in order to be with certain guys who were attracted to me. It was a miserable experience, and I lost a part of myself in that process, mainly because I was too busy trying to please them and not make them look bad.

I can recall getting into arguments with one of my ex-boyfriends in high school because he frequently accused me of making him "look like an idiot". He often said that I acted like I was "running things". I later grew to realize that he battled many insecurities, however, he was an alpha male. He was a hustler- literally, but I didn't know that because I was also a bit naive. He was the leader in his circle.

He was the top guy who his boys went to when they needed help. He was a go-getter and not afraid to stand up for what he believed. However, he was hot-headed, insecure, and very intimidated by my alpha traits. He was a bit controlling, had abusive tendencies, and expected me to basically dumb it down so that I wouldn't embarrass him around his boys and his family. With the type of mother and family I have, those behaviors would've never made it long-term in my life; so that relationship eventually came to an end.

It often took me a while to learn some lessons regarding relationships, because of my naivety. My mother exposed me to many things, but I lived somewhat of a sheltered life which involved me being surrounded by family mainly. Between my family and extracurricular activities, I had very little time to simply hang out as I wanted.

This was actually a good parenting plan until it came to me engaging in relationships with the boys. I missed a lot of those conversations with my peers about boys and my sisters were older with their own family. Oh, and of course I would've never dare to discuss boy problems with my brothers- or with my mom. So, I figured things out the hard way many times through experience.

I didn't understand at that time, but I was really seeking alpha males for dating. Maybe I was seeking males more like my brothers. They all had a combination of common alpha traits, but their personalities varied. Some had aggressive tendencies, then there was the mild mannered older brother, the alpha male boss, who often moved in silence- and far from aggressive. He only gets rowelled up during football season with his friends and family- and that's normally for fun. Well, when I was a senior in high school, I found a combination of an alpha male that landed me in an emotionally abusive relationship. Constant mind games, harassment, stalking, and a lot of controlling was what I dealt with during my senior year that I can't get back. In that relationship, I had stopped walking in my full alpha- as I was raised.

I had become accustomed to dumbing myself down to make the guys I dated look stronger and in charge. Keep in mind, they were initially attracted to me because of my alpha traits. They loved that I was strong, independent, and determined. They needed a smart and resilient female by their side because it looked and felt good. However, to some guys, the alpha female makes them feel as if they're subpar.

So, either they would retreat and find another female whom they could control, or they would try to "break" the strong females and shape them into a world of submissiveness.

Fast forward to my college years, when I met my husband, he was quite the opposite of the alpha males I've previously dated. He didn't try to control or stalk me. He wasn't emotionally abusive either. He was actually my funny and nerdy friend who happened to be quite charming. I didn't look to date him because I wasn't looking to be with anyone after the rough relationship run I had in high school.

However, this dude was different. He was a business student who was well dressed for class nearly every day. I was a nursing student who captured his attention with my tough- yet gentle spirit, my drive for success, my intelligence, and my love for music and comedy. I loved to laugh and he loved making me laugh.

Our dates were different. We had study dates in the library on campus- and we actually studied! He always pushed and challenged me to be better and to go harder; I did the same for him. I drilled him constantly and even made up quizzes for him before he would take a big test. We celebrated our wins by going to the movies or the mall- either together or separately. We were in the Spartan Legion marching band, Jazz band, and Pep band together at Norfolk State University.

We were also Student Ambassadors for the school and gave campus tours to prospects looking to enroll. He landed leadership roles on campus and he was that person everyone seemed to bring their problems to for solving. He was also frequently in the peacekeeper role and often helped to put out fires behind closed doors- yet, he was still the clown of the band and the crew. I, on the other hand, was not quite interested in leadership roles, mainly because I was afraid to step out of my comfort zone. Despite the fear, I was still chosen to take the lead many times on campus for class, in my nursing department, and also in my Army ROTC program.

In addition to those affiliations, we were also in the same work study under the supervision of our band director- who quickly pegged us as a couple despite our denials to ourselves and everyone else. However, we both realized that we made a great team together. I believe this was the beginning of an alpha union- or what we call today, Team Hickman.

Our closest friends would always tell us that we would be amazing when we got married because of our drive individually and together. We were very goal oriented and worked hard for what we wanted. Beyond college, we both had good careers that allowed us leadership and growth opportunities. He began a career in sales management, which led to a career in education, then eventually led to radio programming. He also became very active in the community and is a huge personality in the city. My career in nursing allowed me an opportunity to travel to many cities and states throughout the country. Traveling became an addiction because it provided great opportunities, great pay, and I got to meet new people all the time. However, at times, having a long distance relationship became a challenge.

Eventually, he came and moved me from Virginia Beach, VA to his hometown of Wilmington, NC. We then married a year and a half later. I had a main job, but I also had travel assignments at the same time. So, needless to say, we were both high energy and dedicated people married, but not spending a lot of time together.

We both found ourselves working a lot. We both had two jobs that we were working full-time. What we realized is that we both shared a love for our community and also for helping people.

We also learned that we got bored easily. That is also a characteristic of both alpha males and females. We were always up for a challenge- and we still continue to be. While he currently runs a radio station and is a huge community activist, I no longer work as a travel nurse, nor am I in clinical nursing, but I am an entrepreneur. I stay busy and productive with my coaching practice, mentoring program, creating outlets and platforms for women to heal, and basically building our empire. I often say that I use my stethoscope differently these days and I love it!

As a couple in our city, we are viewed as a powerhouse. We are frequently called a "Power Couple", but we never really saw ourselves as such. We simply decided to follow our dreams and do the things that bring us joy. Individually, we are leaders in our community. We have our own businesses and things we love doing. Then, when we are together, we have our joint ventures and business enterprise we are building. When one of us has an event or a heavier load going on, it impacts the other naturally because we are in the same home.

During this time, we find a balance and the more flexible person would normally fall back just a bit and allow the other to take the lead. Well, I've always been that flexible person to fall back a bit and be the support for my husband when our load became heavier a few years ago. Falling back never meant that my load became easier. It simply meant that I couldn't be in the limelight alongside my husband because I was too busy handling family business. My load actually got much heavier over the years than my husband's load.

Approximately six years ago, we became parents overnight and assumed care of my great nephew full-time. It was not planned as we had nearly a week to prepare for what was to be a summer vacation,. The summer vacation then turned into a year long stay- which then eventually turned to permanent residency. He was coming from an abusive home and needed a new environment that would foster therapeutic development. What a challenge that was to add in the midst of our busy lives, but we have been blessed by his presence, and of course he has been blessed by our's. We have managed to transform his little life and he is simply a reflection of the two alphas grooming him.

At twelve years of age, he does many things that adults wouldn't dare to do- including professional acting, modeling, band, and even cooking a pot roast or a chicken and veggie casserole. His willingness to learn and love, despite his history, has been quite impressive. We have been training him to be a well-rounded servant, a team player, and a go-getter. We are indeed raising him the alpha way.

With a heavier load, it was very important for me to have my own identity. I still had my life and businesses to run, and I also helped to heal a wounded child whom we suddenly acquired care. So, it wasn't like I stopped doing business, but I had to slow down a bit in order to handle the load. This is where my strengths became more pronounced in our relationship.

When I slowed down some, my vision became more clear, and I was able to naturally carry a heavier load than my husband and everyone around me. We still moved together as a team, but I emerged as the silent leader behind the scenes while my husband remained the face seen most in the public's eye.

Together, we simply make things happen and we look like we are having fun doing it. We've been told many times that we make things look easy.

People are always asking us, "how do you do all that you do?" We always laugh it off but reply with a simple answer. It's all God! We are all constantly on the move- whether we are doing speaking engagements, coaching, volunteer work, live events, or traveling for auditions and shows for our child. Amongst all of these things, I still have my hobby-turned-business, where I manually create edible delights, and ship them throughout the country once per month while I seek manufacturing for my products. It truly takes a lot of organization and management skills, patience, determination, and a lot of faith to manage all of this. So, yes, when people ask us how do we do the things we do, we can honestly say that it's nobody but God leading us.

To the average person hearing all that we do, they always say it's a lot and it's exhausting. However, we aren't exhausted by what we do. We are energized by the things we do. What we are doing inspires and impacts our community and beyond, therefore, we continue to be the influencers we were created to be.

There is a popular saying that, "behind every great man is a great woman". Well, it took me years to realize that I am that great woman! It's coming from a place of confidence and knowing exactly what I bring to the table in our relationship and when conducting business.

For example, when we do events or workshops, my husband is actually the bigger personality that shows and helps to bring in the people, but I am the woman behind the scenes running nearly everything and not one to be in the spotlight except when necessary. However, we have reversed roles where he has operated behind the scenes for my events and I was in the limelight.

There is another saying that "a man with dreams needs a woman with vision". Well, I have a natural gifting where I can see the bigger picture and I can also focus in on the fine details. Because of this, I tend to take on the roles of manager, protector, and even the FBI investigator when needed.

This is in addition to me managing nearly everything in the home- including our child and his busy life. I'm always soliciting my husband's help, but I don't always get it- either because of his scheduling, or because he simply doesn't have the capacity and/or skillsets to handle it. Whatever he isn't naturally gifted in, he subconsciously leaves on the plate for me to handle, and I just make it happen.

Now, here is a common issue I've noticed in our relationship when we are planning our annual scholarship fundraiser- which brings in hundreds of guests for a single event. I've been viewed as if I'm ornamental and not functional. Although the event may say Team Hickman, some people would not acknowledge me as the leader or even a partner. They would dismiss me and my efforts and refer to it as my husband's event. They would also attempt to divide us by disrespecting me and discrediting the works I've done. Many times, I encounter these issues from my fellow black females. Despite the fact that my husband repeatedly states that he is just the face and acknowledges that I'm the brains behind the event, some people will bypass me and go directly to him repeatedly to avoid approaching me. Some have even lied and tried to cause friction on our team because they didn't want to accept that I was actually the woman in charge.

With studies showing that women only represent 45% of the S & P 500 workforce, and of that, only 4% are actual CEOs, it's no wonder why I commonly experience friction. People aren't accustomed to seeing women in power. They are accustomed to seeing us alongside a male with power. However, this will require a change of mindset, and we all know that change is not easily accepted by the masses.

Meantime, my husband somehow takes a bit of a beta approach when we are working on an event together that I started, and it irritates me when he does this. He is great at what he does in the community and on his job, but he is not as great at event planning and managing our events. He is the type who will go hard for everyone else except for himself or his brand.

He will subconsciously put himself and his brand last. This makes me irritated and want to fight harder for our team. You see, publicly, we work well together, but I tend to experience a lot of friction behind the scenes when we are working on a big project together. This is simply what I call "the clashing of the alphas".

What do you do when both parties feel they know what's best and need to be in charge? This clashing doesn't last long, but becomes very draining during the process. Eventually, one of us falls back a bit to allow the other to take charge. During this time, our roles become more defined, our strengths are revealed, and we learn a little more about each other. This is when we start to create magic together.

My husband is normally there to support when I ask, but I generally have to ask rather loudly and a few times, then he steps in to help more. I believe this is a result of my actions and old mindset. I was so strong, independent, and resilient, and I never was a damsel in distress type of girl. I was resourceful and would struggle through something alone before asking my husband for assistance.

You see, I had trained my alpha husband to know that, whatever the situation, I had it covered. I somehow had communicated nonverbally to him that I didn't need his help.

The only way to undo this was to simply speak up and state clearly my needs- especially during our demanding event planning collaboration. When I've done this then the beta male disappears and the alpha male re-emerges.

I believe many of us may have alpha males as a mate, but we are so caught up in our alpha that we don't allow them to support us in the way we need.

Sometimes, when we are working together, it may be hard at first to fall back a bit and allow your mate to take the lead. However, I view falling back as a way of simply saying, 'I got your back, Babe'. My husband often jokingly says, "The man is the head of the house." However, as my good friend- and fellow alpha woman always replies, "Yes, that's true, but the woman is the neck, and you can't do nothing without a neck."

Alpha Woman
Powers Activate!

By Suprena Hickman

There was a cartoon in the late 1970's that I recall watching as a child called, the "Wonder Twins". When this dynamic duo was ready to take on a big assignment that required super human strength, they would morph into whatever animal or character they needed to be to get the job done. Prior to their morphing, they always did a united fist bump and stated, "Wonder Twins Powers, Activate!"

They simply became unstoppable until they accomplished their mission. Well, when it comes to the planning of my live events, I definitely activate my alpha woman powers. It literally takes everything that I have in me to pull off amazing events- especially if I'm trying to put hundreds of paid butts in seats, so to speak.

All of the trainings that my momma taught me regarding event planning comes back to me during these times. When I activate my true powers, I become super focused on my mission, and I get easily irritated whenever I encounter anyone trying to take me off of my game.

When I'm operating in my full alpha, I'm usually planning our annual fundraiser which brings hundreds of attendees and is a full blown production. It has so many moving parts and requires a team of strong leaders like myself on board. During my plannings, I've discovered that I need complete control and I need to know what's going on at all times.

I notice nearly everything and my drive is on 100%- even when I want to turn it off. I like to have fun while planning, but I don't tolerate any toxic nonsense. I expect things to be done in order and with excellence and I don't mind removing anyone who will cause friction in my camp.

This isn't the zone for the weak minded and insecure person who requires extra coddling. I also have no toleration for anyone trying to come into my camp and not respecting my vision. By allowing someone to do this, it severely slows down the production and planning process and irritates the heck out of me because it's wasteful.

I naturally get this way because there are so many things at stake if anything goes wrong. When people have said that they wanted to help me with my events, I've found that many times they are inspired by what I do and they aspire to be able to do what I do. However, they don't always possess the skillsets or the drive that I have to be able to assist me in the capacity that they desire.

Because I'm normally in power mode, I don't have time, nor do I desire to create the time, to train anyone while I'm planning. My plate is normally too full and I don't always have enough quality and committed help. You see, many have said they wanted to come onboard, but many aren't really committed to do the work. I've found that people want to come onboard to reap the benefits and attach their name to our brand, but they aren't necessarily prepared to do the actual work required.

Some won't even promote the event unless their names are attached or they can somehow benefit from it. I've experienced very few genuine people wanting to be involved with us in business regarding our events. However, in my experience, the genuine people who actually stick around and do the work longterm, tend to be other alpha females. Our personalities click very well and we are all quite driven. They anticipate my needs while we have fun planning high-impact events.

It takes a certain level of boldness and energy to handle all business needs, like searching for and approaching sponsors and partners. Then, there is the actual planning of the event to include running team meetings and communicating with event participants- like speakers and performers.

Important items like, acquiring the proper resources for decor, food, and drinks are also important details that I have to manage and oversee. Marketing and advertising for the events also requires a different level of energy. Amongst being in charge of these tasks, I also have to make sure the venue is secured and insured.

The normal person, who desires to come onboard and ride the wave, doesn't have to be concerned with these things. I always say, at the end of the day, with any of our events, it's my name and credit card that is on file and on the insurance papers. So, I give myself full permission to activate my alpha woman powers. I've found though, that females who are beast potential, or alpha potential, but are too afraid to walk in their full alpha, are normally the females who will cause the friction and try to compete with me or interrupt my flow.

When conducting business, I've been accused of being aggressive and bossy when I've simply been assertive. I've literally reiterated the same things in a meeting that a male has said and I was labeled as aggressive, bossy, and rude. I was made to feel as if I was too intimidating. Meantime, I noticed those same people who labeled me failed to label my male counterpart who literally said the same thing.

While planning our annual fundraising event a couple of years ago, I remember having a female come to audition for a part, and she was irritated by my mere presence onsite. She questioned my volunteers as to why I was present with some of the planning. She stated that this was not my event, but it was my husband's event.

You see, the lack of acknowledgment for my existence would always come off as disrespectful and irritating to me. I've been verbally attacked during the planning of nearly every huge and impactful event that we've had. That simply becomes quite draining over time.

During those times, I often questioned myself and asked others in my circle to pay more attention to the dynamics on the team- without my saying what specific issues I've experienced. I simply wanted to know if it was me speaking harshly or what they felt I was dealing with. I really began to think harshly of myself, but thank God it was only briefly.

Well, to my surprise, they said no it was not me. I've had others, who witnessed the backlash I received from me activating my alpha woman powers, encourage me to keep going. They told me that this was their insecurities and that wasn't my problem. I had to learn how to move forward from the backlash so that my negative thoughts wouldn't be in the way of my success. I've never experienced an attack from the males, but they would naturally bypass me and go to my husband and ask questions or to get information regarding our events.

I've had a male preacher approach my husband and I about our annual event, but he never once looked at me. He only spoke to my husband. When my husband was speaking, he did reference "we", as to include me, however, that didn't change the preacher's approach.

Meantime, after the conversation ended, I clarified some things with my husband about the event and mentioned how I felt disrespected by the action. Of course, there was nothing that could be done at that point, so nothing else came of it. In the Bible, it states that the man is the head of the house, so I guess people are likely going to whomever they feel is naturally in charge. For many, it just doesn't happen to be the woman.

Needless to say, I've learned to be assertive after being walked over, disrespected, and misinterpreted. I stopped worrying about stepping on toes or being too bold when I'm doing business. I stopped being afraid to approach people thinking I may be too aggressive. I also stopped being afraid to take control of situations when I can see the bigger picture.

The things that have always kept me focused on the bigger picture is knowing my purpose and realizing that what I do is so much greater than me. I'm called to help heal emotional wounds so people could focus more on their purpose in life. I'm called to serve mainly women and help them focus more on taking out time for themselves. In that process is when they would further define their purpose and begin to take action.

If I'm not doing this through coaching and empowerment workshops/conferences, then I'm doing it through other creative events in a form of edutainment. It's a combination of educating and entertaining to deliver the messages you desire to get to your audience.

Our annual fundraiser is an example of edutainment that I created eight years ago to help my husband heal from the sudden loss of his mom- who was an educator of forty years. My husband became very depressed as a result of her passing, and he was in denial of his behaviors and feelings.

The event I created was a scholarship fundraiser in the form of a fashion show similar to a larger known fashion show on BET at that time. Our show featured indie artists, designers, models, and local community who's who. Just imagine the personalities I've dealt with and the amount of energy that was required to produce this show.

In the beginning, the branding was not highlighting the scholarship, but instead, it highlighted my husband as the local celebrity in the city having a fashion show. This brought on many groupies and people who didn't respect my vision. Everything promoting the event was all geared toward the club-goers appeal. The graphic designers focused more on big booty and breasted girls with my husband featured in the middle of the flyer. It took me going through many challenges, as I stated earlier, to get to a point where I could change the trajectory of the event to a more positive light. This process required me to take massive action as I felt that my vision was being stolen away from me. I knew God gave it to me to help my husband heal and I knew a change had to happen and quickly.

The change process required some purging. I started purging from the team on down to the mindsets of those around us and assisting us. This action did not come without any friction from my husband. However, I activated my alpha woman powers and stood my ground. I worked around him and everyone else who seemed to be what I saw as a road block to keep my vision from manifesting.

There were times when I felt that nearly my entire team and my husband was against me, but I persevered. Eventually, the change started to occur, but it wasn't big enough to get a diverse community feel present. So, one year, I decided to show people who my husband really was. I sought out and approached people like the sheriff, state senator, a lead news anchor, the mayor, presidents of key community organizations, a pro football player, and so much more. These were people he actually had a relationship with and communicated regularly to. They called on him for various needs in the community frequently throughout the year. So, I thought they needed to be a part of something my husband regarded as important to him.

I invited them to be models in the show and explained to them why they needed to be there. They actually said yes. I created a local celebrity scene and it caused many newbies to attend our show. I knew that if these people could simply attend, then they would see the great works we were doing and would be of great support going forward.

Well, that's exactly what happened. I also made it mainly a surprise for my husband. He only knew of two to three local celebrities who were modeling, yet, when the event occurred, everyone gave him credit for bringing out the city's local celebrities to the show. I invited nearly twenty of them! It made the news, local magazines, and newspaper and was highlighted for nearly three weeks in media outlets.

The city was talking about the event I created for my husband to help him heal from a depressive state. During the show, I got the local celebrities' attire, hair, and makeup sponsored, and they had a blast. I made sure to include them in the shout outs on social media and I even created a personalized flyer to promote on their page. This brought more awareness to the event and it also brought in more funds for the scholarship.

Finally, people were acknowledging our event as scholarship fund in honor of his late mom. People started focusing more on education, community, and the power of healing from depression.

It was this moment when I realized how much I actually influenced my husband. You see, he started speaking out about depression, and the importance of recognizing the signs, then getting some help. That was a huge moment for me seeing my proud, black alpha male of a husband on stage before hundreds of predominantly black people and acknowledging his battle with depression.

Talking about his experience with depression has brought on many conversations about it with others in the community. The local hospital wanted to be a part of the event and help with the movement as well. Yes, I created a movement of people uniting in the community to support each other in their businesses, their purpose, pushing out of their comfort zones, and helping students go to college. All of this started from the need to heal. That is purposeful living.

I never expected it to be as large as it has grown to be. However, this process is part of what has shaped me into the alpha woman I am today. It took purpose, perseverance, poise, and pressure to bring forth the profits.

Today, in addition to heading the scholarship fundraising event that we produce annually, remember I empower women and teen girls and help them heal from their emotional wounds and gain more confidence to pursue their purpose. I have an event-based women's organization that I created a few years ago to give women a platform to use their gifts and to promote themselves.

I'm very passionate about helping up-and-coming women. Therefore, I create space where women could come and enjoy themselves while they connect with other powerful women making moves. There is also room for the woman who hasn't quite come out of her shell and desires to be around the alpha woman.

In my experience, alpha women attract alpha women. We understand each other and we energize each other. When we unite or collaborate for business, there is no room to be petty and immature. There is no jealousy or envy either. We are simply too busy creating and living out our purpose- oh and we definitely want to bring other women along with us for the ride.

However, while on this journey of empowering women, I realized the hard way that everyone cannot go with you. Sometimes, we have to know when to allow that elevator door to open and let people get off at the level where they are most comfortable or can function.

Hard learned lessons on this journey have been quite time consuming and rather expensive. I've spent too much time over the years trying to bring other women along with me and make them see what I see. I commonly say that I have a dream, just as our beloved alpha male, Dr. Martin Luther King, Jr. did.

I have a dream that one day, we will have millions of healed women uniting and collaborating to help heal and nurture our young girls. The key word here is "healed" women. The problem has been that many women stopped working on themselves and they become emotionally toxic. I've been there as well, so I understand this cycle. Someone hurts us very badly, then we lose confidence and we begin to somehow lose a sense of direction. We forget who we truly are and what we are called to do. We simply lose interest.

Then, we stop reaching for our goals because we start to feel a bit hopeless. We literally stop walking in our alpha. It happens! Well, just as I had a strong alpha woman who fearlessly activated her alpha woman powers to help me, I want to be that same alpha woman for other women in need. As they begin to heal, they will re-activate their alpha woman powers.

At this point, if they have young girls, then they will naturally pass on new behaviors to them and foster a new cycle of healing. I thoroughly enjoy going through this process with the women. I especially love when they start to do the work and become more radiant. I love seeing an alpha woman activate her powers because she becomes fearless beyond measure.

Oh, and seeing a young alpha girl walk in her alpha is amazing as well. However, I have a little soft spot for that young alpha girl who is still yet learning how to walk in her alpha- just as I had to.

So, this brings me to my teen mentoring program for girls. I started this program a few years ago to address the needs of the teen girls dealing with low self-esteem who simply needed mentoring. However, studies have shown that one in three young people will grow up without a mentor in their life and I simply desire to help bridge that gap.

The National Mentoring Partnership has shown that for our at-risk youth who have had mentoring, they are 130% more likely to hold leadership positions. I feel it's important for them to be exposed to things they aren't normally familiar with at their age. I enjoy every moment of witnessing their transformation. To address their needs, and help build their confidence level, I hold monthly workshops for them.

The problems I've encountered most were from teen girls with parents who viewed my organization as if it were a social club and they weren't fully vested. During those times, I had girls who came to the monthly sessions late or whenever they wanted. They also arrived constantly sleepy and hungry. The parents were very busy working and didn't pay much attention to their kids as they should have.

Their cellphones were the babysitters and a huge distraction in their life. When I would insert assertiveness, some of the kids would exhibit toxic behaviors towards me. I also experienced the same from their parents- if not worse.

During this time, I also had females who signed up to assist me in my efforts as a volunteer mentor, but some simply lacked clarity on their purpose and therefore, they had little drive. They also lacked consistency, and that is something much needed when working with kids.

I continued to simply make it work and tolerate the behaviors, but it didn't work in my favor. The vibes weren't right amongst my mentors and business partner and the kids could feel it also.

One day, it seemed as if all of my volunteers were no longer available. Eventually, they all walked away for various reasons. They all left except one woman. The healed, alpha woman stayed- and is still here. Just as I mentioned earlier about the purging in regards to changing the trajectory of our scholarship fund, this is what happened with my teen mentoring organization. The only exception is that I didn't do the purging. It was done for me. During the abandonment season, I thought many times about quitting, but I had girls who were depending on me to show up. So, I became more driven and I focused more on my purpose. It's a skill I've acquired over the years for every time I've felt like giving up.

It never fails me to focus more on my purpose. The blessing after the abandonment is that I started to attract more alpha women who were dedicated and believed in what I was doing. They came in offering quality and consistent service and soon the quality of girls changed as well.

I have girls who are now ambassadors and they are recruiting other like-minded girls to become a member of their organization. Yes, I said their organization, because they have taken ownership and it shows in their actions.

So, I now have a smaller group of ambitious teen girls who are ready to explore and be mentored. They are leaders and they bring amazing energy. The mindsets and behaviors of the parents are different and more inviting as well. Again, alpha women attract alpha women, so naturally the teen girls would follow the light that we give off. These experiences, have reminded me to go harder for my vision- no matter what happens. Giving up is simply not an option.

We activate our alpha woman powers when we are living out our purpose and when we are mission focused. When we do this, the other alphas will find us, and greatness occurs.

Meet The Alpha Women Experts

Dr. Shekina Farr Moore

Dr. Shekina Farr Moore is a scholar, a thought leader and the visionary behind the <u>Miseducation of the Alpha Woman</u> Anthology.

Named among Atlanta's Power 25, Dr. Shekina Farr Moore, Ed.D, is an Author, Gender Advocate, Master Certified Coach (MCC) and **FORBES Coaches Council** Member.

She is also Co-CEO of Eroom Marketing Group, an empowerment parent company that oversees Intercontinental Coaching Institute, Fierce Academy, Literacy Moguls Publishing, Black Reins Magazine (the first and only black cowboy magazine in the southeast), Formidable Woman Magazine, ZOOM CON (featured on the White House's *United State of Women* in 2016) and her Non-profit, B2F Girls Worldwide--a gender empowerment incubator that offers a comprehensive certification and accreditation program and produces advocacy initiatives, campaigns and events.

She has spoken out against gender oppression and disempowerment since 1992, penning her first published article, "Blocking Out the Gender Gap", while a high school student. This article garnered the attention of the National Press for Women. She is also the author of eighteen empowerment books including: Blah to Fierce: Women's 30-Day Guide to Getting Unstuck; Beautiful, Big-boned and Brown; Black Girls Hear: Untold Stories of the Marginalized, Unsafe & Unwelcomed; and co-author of When Dark Chocolate is Bittersweet: Controversy Within A Culture.

Dr. Moore has received many national and community awards for her work with social justice and gender advocacy, including the **Volunteer Service Award signed by President Barack Obama** and a standing ovation and resolution by the GA House of Representatives.

In 2016 and 2017, Dr. Moore was named among **Atlanta's "Who's Who"** and **Atlanta's "Power 25"**, and was recognized as one of "**52**

Empowering Women Who Empower Girls" in 2014. In 016 she received the Humanitarian Award and the WEN Diamond Award for women in business. In 2017 Dr. Moore was honored with the **SOAR Award** at Amplify Her Life Atlanta. In 2018 she was named "Leading Lady" by Miz CEO Magazine and received the distinguished **Community Impact Award** from Solo Moms Foundation.

In March 2019 she was named **Educator of the Year** by ACHI Magazine. She has been featured for her work in gender advocacy by many publications, including **Forbes, Black Enterprise, The Huffington Post, SHEEN**, **Rolling Out**, Millennial Mom, Courageous Woman, Today's Purpose Woman, Connected Woman, Head2Toe, MizCEO and more.

Dr. Moore earned her B.A. in French (1999) and her M.S.A. in School Administration from North Carolina Central University (2004). She earned her Ed.S. (2009) and her Ed.D. (2016) in Educational Administration and Supervision from North Carolina State University.

Her doctoral research focused on the perspectives of Black male teachers and the recruitment strategies employed by colleges, universities and local education agencies. This garnered the attention of many, including The

Twenty-sixth International Learners
Conference 2019 and The National
Conference on Education where Dr. Moore
was asked by the School Superintendent's
Association (AASA) to present her data to and
lead discourse with state superintendents from
around the country.

Dr. Moore is a member of Lean In Atlanta, the
National Association for Multicultural
Education and the National Association of
Professional Women. Her **Fierce to
Formidable** movement is empowering women
to *unbecome* everything that is not really them.

She enjoys family time, cooking, and binge-
reading with a good, hot green tea and sushi.

For booking Inquiries, contact:
info@B2Fgirls.org.

www.traintocoach.com
www.formidablewomanmag.com
|www.B2Fgirls.org

Aisha N. Martin

Aisha Martin, a nurturer by nature, is a cultured, creative, powerhouse with a youthful spirit and personable demeanor. Raised and educated primarily in Europe she has combined her artistic gifts, global travel, and experiences as a seasoned biologist with her heart for inspiring girls to be authentic, confident STEM leaders. Aisha's STEM journey spans almost a decade and began at the Centers for Disease Control in Atlanta, GA as a Molecular Biologist. She has held positions at Emory University Medical School, the Georgia Public Health Lab, and Baylor-Miraca Genetics Lab. As a certified Girls Empowerment Coach and STEMinist, her vision is to close the "gender gap to innovation," by engaging girls from underserved and historically underrepresented communities through early exposure to STEM education and specialized mentoring. Aisha holds a Bachelor of Science (BS) in Biology from Clark Atlanta University and a Master of Science in Forensic Science (MSFS) from National University.

Aisha's mantra is "girls can't be what they don't see!" Her experiences as a female scientist in a male-dominated industry, coupled with her frustration at the lack of female STEM role models and mentors were the inspiration behind Fems4STEM™ which she founded in 2015. Aisha saw the need for early exposure to STEM through hands-on activities and resources to ensure that girls are successful and competitive in STEM.

More importantly, a void needed to be filled in terms of female mentorship to combat the lack of gender diversity in STEM professions. She found that if more girls were exposed to STEM with the support of a female mentor on a consistent basis and with whom they could identify, they were more likely to pursue a STEM degree and career. Fems4STEM™ is on a mission to empower, inspire and equip a nation of girls with the knowledge; skills and confidence to be global STEM leaders.

She has been featured in Connected Woman Magazine and Formidable Woman Magazine. She was a contributing author in the Black Girls Hear Anthology for which she was honored with a Community Impact Award from Literacy Moguls Publishing sponsored by Sheen Magazine.

She is a co-author of the critically acclaimed anthology Letters to Our Daughters. Aisha was recognized at the 2015 Tween Star Awards™ as a Mentoring Star and honored with the Presidential Volunteer Service Award signed by U.S. President Barack Obama for her passion and dedication to mentoring girls. She has also been a featured guest on Connecting Atlanta Radio powered by World Star Hit Radio.

Aisha's global travel and experiences lend themselves well to her role overseeing Organizational Partnerships, Charitable Donations, Fundraisers, Sponsorship, Community Involvement, & Research Implementation for the Tween Star Awards™ a national recognition platform for girls.

She is also a proud volunteer at sister organization B2F Girls™ assisting in various capacities to facilitate their mission of "empowering one million girls with healthy esteem and unapologetic fierce!"

She currently resides in Orlando, FL with her husband Ricardo and two future global leaders, her son Shai ("Shy") and daughter Sade ("Shah-day").

When she's not empowering girls globally to pursue STEM, Aisha enjoys traveling, cooking, performing arts, writing, reading and spending quality time with family and friends.

Dr. Barbara L. Swinney

Coach, Speaker, Author

An educational leader of more than 20 years, Dr. Swinney has served teachers, students, parents, business leaders, and communities in her role as a classroom teacher, principal, and Assistant Superintendent.

She has collaborated with board members, county commissioners, state representatives, and district and local school leaders to ensure improved teaching and learning in an effort to promote the future health and wealth of the total school community. Her career has allowed her to support leaders in establishing and clarifying their vision and aligning goals so that they are able to expand their capacity to serve their communities and live their purpose from any position.

Combining her experience as a leader, her gifts as a visionary, and her ability to inspire others to see things differently, Dr. Swinney founded Barbara Swinney, INC., Life and Leadership Coaching Firm. She is a John Maxwell Certified Life Coach for Leaders, Speaker, Teacher, and Author of, "It's Always DEEPER: Six Steps to Achieving Perpetual Success".

Dr. Swinney has been featured in publications such as Sheen Magazine, Today's Purpose Woman Magazine, Bold Favor Magazine, Connected Woman Magazine, and Formidable Woman Magazine.

Dr. Swinney focuses on holistic leadership, the personal and professional success of leaders; and helping driven people live a more fulfilled life by inspiring transformational thinking, leadership, and personal growth.

Though her experience has been vast and essential to the evolution of educational leadership, Dr. Swinney considers her most important work to be raising her two daughters. She balances her work life by spending time with her family and playing tennis with her Championship Tennis Team.

Dr. Koyah Alston

Dr. Koyah, known as "the driven professor", is a sought-after motivational speaker and author who received dual Bachelor of Arts degrees in English and Communication Studies from The University of North Carolina at Wilmington. Dr. Alston also attended North Carolina Agricultural and Technical State University, where she earned a Master of Science degree in Adult Education with a concentration in English Teaching and a Doctor of Philosophy in Leadership Studies.

Before beginning her professional career, Dr. Alston founded Student Body Television (now Teal-TV) at The University of North Carolina at Wilmington shortly after landing a full-time role as the Morning TV Writer/Producer of "Carolina in the Morning" at WECT-TV, the NBC television station in Wilmington, North Carolina.

She went on to work in television in numerous capacities as a national TV Host, TV Producer/Writer, and even as the President of her own Media Production Company.

After broadening her reach to educational terrains, Dr. Alston followed her passion for education through launching her teaching career as English Teacher to at-risk high school students and then as a Language Arts Teacher/Track & Cheerleading Coach for the Wake County Public School System before transitioning to the field of higher education in a college admissions role at Shaw University.

For over 7 years, she also worked in a variety of program management capacities at The University of North Carolina at Chapel Hill, including Pre-College Outreach Coordinator for the North Carolina Health Careers Access Program (NC-HCAP), Registrar/Manager of Advanced Education Programs for UNC School of Dentistry, and the Assistant Director of the Undergraduate Business Program for UNC's Kenan-Flagler School of Business.

Dr. Alston is currently an Adjunct Professor of English and Humanities at various postsecondary institutions and is often called upon as a motivational speaker to speak on a variety of leadership and empowerment topics to K-20 students and to present on health disparities and the lack of minority presence in the health professions.

LaToya Rose

LaToya Rose is a native of Tulsa, Oklahoma—a wealthy city built on the principles of Christ, community, and commerce with its unbreakable Black Wall Street District.

During her younger years, LaToya Rose leveraged entrepreneurship and community service to combat the anguish she suffered from experiencing sexual traumas at age five. She found peace and joy with baking and began selling cookies from her Easy Bake Oven to the neighborhood kids.

LaToya Rose began working various corporate jobs at age fourteen, from working the drive-thru on Pine and Peoria, to retail and telecommunications before realizing her desires of full-time entrepreneurship in 2016. She found herself at a pivotal point during this time where she would either choose to continue to work just to earn a paycheck with limited incentives or she could transfer her skills and knowledge to create her own economy.

LaToya Rose is on a mission. To her core, she is concerned with helping people discover their genius, create strong partnerships, and monetize their expertise. She is graduate of Langston University (Bachelor of Science) & North Carolina Central University (Master of Education).

She started preparing taxes in 2005 to help her college associates claim their education refundable credits. With time and leadership as an Office Manager of a national tax company, she soon found her true desires for a career in tax preparation and debt resolution.

Currently, she is the Owner and Senior Tax Accountant of Rose Tax Solutions- boutique tax firm on Historic Greenwood Avenue. Her community involvement includes facilitating the global vision of the Black Wall Street Exchange, volunteering her administration skills for a National Law Literacy program, and mentoring students in the Tulsa Public School district.

LaToya Rose is a Mother, Business Owner, Public Speaker, Facilitator of Shift, Community Leader, and Published author (Money Matters: Life After Graduation, Rise & Grind, and A Mother's Love).

She knows arriving to your golden years on a fixed income is no way to live when you can help it. Life has taught her "everyone has a calling and it's proper to find a common ground to foster healing, peace, development and growth." LaToya Rose knows that when you put God in all you do, everything flourishes without question.

Shontavia Hornsby

Shontavia Hornsby is a best-selling Author, Entrepreneur, and Founder and CEO of Raising a Diamond where she is a certified girl's empowerment and life coach.

With 20 years of corporate and professional work experience and inspired by her own youth experience. Shontavia founded Raising a Diamond organization to empower young girls through education, peer mentoring, enhancing self esteem, leadership opportunities.

Shontavia is a passionate communicator and girls empowerment enthusiast who is making a positive impact in the lives of girls, young women, and the people who care about them.

Shontavia holds a B.A. (1996) in Political Science from Prairie View A&M University and a M.S. (2013) in Strategic Leadership from Mountain State University.

Shontavia believes in serving and community involvement. She has been a dedicated volunteer with Meals on Wheels for over 16 years. Shontavia is also a proud member of Alpha Kappa Alpha Sorority, Inc. where she serves in leadership position and works actively the in community providing service to all mankind.

It is her mission to inspire a generation of women who interact with one another on these bases, and whose self- esteem, leadership, and commitment to giving back set an example for the generations of women who follow them. Shontavia believes there are three key elements to the development of confident young females.

Find a passion- do something that inspires you, have a mentor- someone to encourage and guide you in your path, and have a purpose- stand for something that's a cause outside of self and actively support. Raising a Diamond is the embodiment of these beliefs in action. Shontavia, Raising a Diamond girls mentor organization is active in the community, and have partnered with schools to provide a school-based mentoring program.

Shontavia has been featured in Formidable Woman Magazine, Today's Purpose Woman Magazine, and Today's Purpose Woman 2018 Calendar. She also co-authored a best seller anthology, Letters to Our Daughters.

She currently resides in Austin, TX. When she is not empowering girls to pursue their greatness. Shontavia enjoys traveling, reading, spending quality time with family and friends.

www.ShontaviaHornsby.com
www.RaisingaDiamond.com

Stephanie A.

Stephanie A. is easily described as a breath of fresh air! She moves with a humble certainty about herself and the qualities that she brings to the table. As the first lady pioneer of her business Emerging – Butterflies, she can be found inspiring people from all walks of life as she positions herself to be a well-recognized self –love motivational empowerment speaker.

As an Author she gives a refreshing perspective that allows her readers to find a personal place of connection in her written work. Calling the many who follow to step out of the mind set of being stuck. She actively seeks to empower her coaching clients and encourages them to move forward in their greatness!

She is the Self-Love Trainer that we have been waiting for who embodies the hunger and works of a true Alpha Woman. She moves confidently in her working career as a power house school operations administrator, carefully articulating the required framework for the masses.

She oozes with light and amazing energy and can often be found singing to her own tune when she is happy. While she values all of life's purpose and favor, being a mother is her greatest reward. She strives daily to be the truest example of grace, determination, balance and leadership. She is a walking example that Milwaukee, Wisconsin can produce amazing fruit!

Suprena Hickman

Suprena Hickman is the founder and CEO of Suprena Hickman Enterprises- which consists of three divisions: SHE Wellness (Escape 2 Sisterhood and Girls Rocking In The South- GRITS), Sweet Escapes By Suprena, and Your Escape Coach which is a personal development and wellness company ultimately focusing on self-care.

Suprena, a wife, mother, & passionate community leader, earned her B.S. in Nursing from Norfolk State University and her M.B.A from the University of Phoenix. In addition to being a Registered Nurse, she is a Certified Integrative Health Coach through Duke Integrative Medicine.

She has a passion for helping women heal from their past hurts in order to fearlessly pursue their passion and purpose. She does this through coaching, private retreats, and workshops. Mrs. Hickman is married and currently raising her nephew- who does acting, modeling, and is in the band in school.

She has worked hard to ensure her identity is not lost in the shadows of her child or busy husband who is a local radio programmer, on-air personality, and popular community leader. She manages to build her empire while supporting her family and community. She also works with her husband to create and promote impactful, quality events for their community.

Suprena has experienced her share of hurts and has learned the beautiful art of healing. Now, she uses her past and current experiences, her gift of discernment and coaching, along with her nearly 20 years of professional Nursing expertise to help others heal- as she has, and continues to do.

She affectionately says that she uses her stethoscope differently these days- and she loves it! Suprena understands what it looks and feels like being in toxic environments and relationships. Therefore, she has a passion for helping women heal from their past hurts in order to fearlessly pursue their passion and purpose.

"There are some people who still feel threatened by strong women. That's their problem. It's not mine."

-Gloria Allred

REFERENCES

Alston, K.D. (2018). Strive, Survive, and Thrive: A phenomenological study to understand perceived factors affecting African Americans' career advancement into leadership roles in academic medicine (Doctoral dissertation). (Order No. 10955). Accepted by ProQuest Dissertations & Theses Global.

Association of American Medical Colleges. (2016a). An overview of women full-time medical school faculty of color. *AAMC Faculty Roster, 16*(4). Washington, DC: Author.Retrieved from https://www.aamc.org/download/460728/data/ may2016 anoverviewofwomenfull-imemedicalschoolfacultyofcolor.pdf

Association of American Medical Colleges. (2017). *Table C: Department chairs by department, sex, and race/ethnicity, 2017*. Washington, DC: Author.

Brown, Lachlan (2017, December 23). Women with alpha personalities have these 15 special traits. Retrieved from URL.

Carnes, M., Bartels, C. M., Isaac, C., Kaatz, A., & Kolehmainen, C. (2015). Why is John more likely to become department chair than Jennifer? *Transactions of the American Clinical & Climatological Association, 126,* 197–213.

Epstein, N. E. (2017). Discrimination against female surgeons is still alive: Where are the full professorships and chairs of departments? *Surgical Neurology International, 8,* 93. doi:10.4103/sni.sni_90_17

Hamilton, R. H. (2016). Enhancing diversity in academic neurology: From agnosia to action.

Annals of Neurology, 79(5), 705–708.

Jackson, J. F. L. (2004). Introduction: A crisis at the top: A national perspective. *Journal of Negro Education, 73*(1), 1–3. doi:10.2307/3211255

Mazzoni, M. (2018). Only two fortune 500 ceo's are women of color. What's up with that? Retrieved at:https://www.triplepundit.com/story/2018/only-two-fortune-500-ceos-are-women-color-whats/11146

McDaniel, K. (2017). Medical schools need still more women in leadership. *Health Progress, September-October,* 17–19. Retrieved from https://www.chausa.org/publications/health- progress/article/september-october-2017/medical-schools-need-still-more-women-in- leadership

Morin, Amy (2016, August 4). 7 Ways Women Can Thrive In A Male-Dominated Workplace. Retrieved from URL.

Promoting the advancement of minority women faculty in academic medicine. The National Centers of Excellence in Women's Health. Journal of Women's Health & Gender-based Medicine, 10(6), 541–550.

Rhodes, Sonya PhD. "Alpha women, Beta woman." Psychology Today. April 12, 2014

Rodríguez, J. E., Campbell, K. M., & Mouratidis, R. W. (2014). Where are the rest of us?

Improving representation of minority faculty in academic medicine. *Southern Medical Journal, 107*(12), 739–744. doi:10.14423/SMJ.0000000000000204

Van Edwards, Vanessa (n.d.). The Alpha Female: 9 Ways You Can Tell Who is an Alpha Woman. Retrieved from URL

Walker, Angela (n.d.). 10 Serious Challenges Alpha Women Face. Retrieved from URL.

Ward, R. M., DiPaolo, D. G., Posposon, H.C. (2009). College student leaders: Meet the alpha female. *Journal of Educational Leadership*, 7, 100-117.

Ward, R. M., DiPaolo, D. G., Posposon, H.C. (2010). Defining the alpha female: A female leadership measure. *Journal of Leadership and Organizational Studies*, 7 (3), 309-320.

Wesley, Andrea (n.d.). Why An Alpha Female Is The Best Girlfriend You'll Ever Have. Retrieved from URL.

Whyte, Chelsea (2018, September 26). The 7 non-human mammals where females rule the roost. Retrieved from URL.

Winter, Catherine (2018, September 14). 8 Things An Alpha Woman Brings To A Relationship. Retrieved from URL. Morin, Amy (2016, August 4). 7 Ways Women Can Thrive In A Male-Dominated Workplace. Retrieved from URL.

Woods, L. A., Wetle, T. F., & Sharkey, K. M. (2018). Why aren't more women in academic medicine reaching the top? Rhode Island Medical Journal, 101(3), 19–21.

Wong, E. Y., Bigby, J., Kleinpeter, M., Mitchell, J., Camacho, D., Dan, A., & Sarto, G. (2001).

Yu, P. T., Parsa, P. V., Hassanein, O., Rogers, S. O., & Chang, D. C. (2013). Minorities struggle to advance in academic medicine: A 12-year review of diversity at the highest levels of America's teaching institutions. Journal of Surgical Research, 182(2), 212–218. doi:10.1016/j.jss.2012.06.049

More Anthologies

Available on Amazon

Black Girls Hear

Letters to Our Daughters

MISEDUCATION
OF THE
ALPHA WOMAN

Learn more about

Miseducation of the

Alpha Woman

at

www.B2Fgirls.org

www.ingramcontent.com/pod-product-compliance
Lightning Source LLC
Chambersburg PA
CBHW062212270326
41930CB00009B/1714